P9-CJY-189

AN ANGLER'S ANTHOLOGY

AN ANGLER'S ANTHOLOGY

EDITED BY EUGENE BURNS

ILLUSTRATED BY LOUIS MACOUILLARD

THE STACKPOLE COMPANY   •   HARRISBURG, PENNSYLVANIA

Copyright 1952

By The Telegraph Press

All Rights Reserved

Printed in the U.S.A.

By THE TELEGRAPH PRESS

Established 1831

Harrisburg, Pennsylvania

In The Remembrance Of...

A fishing trip when I lived again,
A dogwood halo'd in bright sunlight,
Trout and mint julep by a cold spring,
Candy-striped Lewisia, at a deer fording,
An "artificial hatch" with a rainbow swirling,
The pervading memory of Joe Campbell on the Claiborne,
A glass or two of friendship mixed with 15-2 and his nob make 3,
An invitation, never-to-be-forgotten: "Come, fish with us in Norway,"
The murmured benediction of the McCloud with deep sleep attending.

    To go with all this, a cheerful band of fishing friends:
Jane and Al; Frank, Kay and Marj; Ann, Bobby, Bill and Polly;
and my host, and friend, Dan Volkmann, who kept reminding:
"Take it easy, Gene, there'll always be good fishing tomorrow."

v

Books by Eugene Burns

THEN THERE WAS ONE

THE LAST KING OF PARADISE

FRESH AND SALT WATER SPINNING

Contents

The Angler

The Boy

The Fish

The Great Old Fish

The Tranquility

Pleasures Attending

Weather & When To Angle

The Water

Methods Precepts & Admonishments

Fly Fishing

Companionship

Tall Tales

Night Fishing

Fishing Tackle

Bait & Flies

Fish On The Table

Food & Lodging

The Bookshelf

A Statement to the Reader:

ONE OF THE abiding pleasures of angling is the fine literature that goes along with it. Anglers read and write as no other sportsmen do.

This collection is what I like best in angling literature and it was put together to pass on to others part of the delight I found in working with the originals.

Such a book seems particularly needful today when the emphasis is entirely too much away from blue skies and sparkling brooks and upon the scientific streamlining of our recreation. With it, that pleasant accompaniment of angling, conversation, has too frequently lapsed into the jargon of a mere hobby: tapered leaders measured with micrometers, tetracarbonchloride mixed with Mucilin for dressing, chemical hand warmers, magnetized dry fly boxes, HCG torpedo-head tapered shooting lines, automatic reels, glass fibre rods, plastic creels, and daylight fluorescent trout flies! To go with the mechanical array there are liver-fed hatchery-reared trout, cross-bred of course, who wouldn't know how to address a caddis should they ever meet one face to face in a stream.

There is a real need for a return to the quietness and tranquility of the stream—and much of this, I think, can be found in angling's happy literature.

An Angler's Anthology began thirty years ago when I first underscored passages of Izaak Walton's *Compleat Angler* and stained its leaves by pressing apple blossoms, trilliums and bluebells between them. It came to full flower when I abandoned my studies in the old halls where Thoreau once went to school, and stuffed myself instead with the wonderful writings of the old anglers—Mascall, Taverner, Markham, Walton & Cotton, Howlett, Chetham, Scope—in the fabulous Fearing collection of angling books in

Widener Memorial library, Harvard, with that unpretentious angler, Robert H. Haynes, assistant librarian, pointing out to me the likely passages where great stories might be landed. No one could have asked for a better guide.

But the high point came wholly unexpectedly one day—as a great fish sometimes swirls at the fly when least looked for in a small pool—not in the great Fearing collection. It was among the college's Anglo-Saxon stacks: Aelfric's *Colloquy* in which I found *The Fisher,* a rare discovery, really, because it is again as old as the oldest recognized piece on angling written in England! It goes back to about 1000 A.D. while heretofore the oldest accepted piece was *The Treatyse of Fysshynge Wyth an Angle* in the Boke of St. Albans, first edition, 1486. *The Fisher,* Colloquy No. 53, a conversational question and answer lesson between teacher and pupil was compiled by Aelfric, Archbishop of Canterbury, who lived sometime between 955 and 1020 A.D. and he used it to instruct his Anglo-Saxon scholars in Latin.

An Angler's Anthology is full of old and new. After what may be the oldest piece on that "huge and cumbersome" fish, the salmon, by Gervase Markham, it presents the Lazy S, a brand new cast which helps the dry fly angler put down that perfect float which is at once the delight and despair of the flycaster.

It was my hope that with a good sprinkling of Izaak Walton, his quiet, gentle philosophy mixed with good humor and piety would pervade the entire book.

Accomplished angler that Walton must have been, he borrowed heavily for his *Compleat Angler,* 1653, from Leonard Mascall's *A Booke of Fishing with Hooke and Line,* 1590, and from Gervase Markham's *Country Contentments,* 1614, and these men in turn worked over the material presented in the *Boke of St. Albans,* 1496, and who knows where that material came from. Certainly, no recreation ever sprang from the earth so full-grown! But recognizing his own shortcomings in fly fishing, Walton called upon his fishing companion, Charles Cotton, to write a second part for his fifth edition, 1676, the last during his lifetime although it has since gone through more than 150 editions

In *An Angler's Anthology* the reader will find that a contemporary of Walton, Richard Franck, who marched with Cromwell while Izaak the churchman followed the king, took him to task saying that Walton was ". . . to be pitied, poor man, for his loss of time, in scribling and transcribing other men's notions . . ." This, today, is the only reason why Franck appears in our pages.

Curiously, the first description I have encountered of dry fly fishing, as such, came from the quill of one of America's foremost authors and not at all an accomplished angler—our own beloved creator of Rip van Winkle and Ichabod Crane, Washington Irving, who described a peg-legged angler he met while strolling along the banks of the Alun, which flows into the Dee, in England. This man, followed by two young beginners, wrote Irving, ". . . stumped from one part of the brook to another; waving his rod in the air . . . and the adroitness with which he would throw his fly to any particular place; sometimes skimming it lightly along a little rapid; sometimes casting it into one of those dark holes made by a twisted root or overhanging bank, in which the large trout are apt to lurk. In the meanwhile he was giving instructions to his two disciples; showing them the manner in which they should handle their rods, fix their flies, and play them along the surface of the stream." This was 1820. And yet some authorities say dry fly fishing is less than sixty years old.

For curiosity's sake, I have included excerpts from such men as Samuel Pepys, George Washington, John James Audubon, Samuel Johnson, Lord Byron, and Grover Cleveland but holding them down to a minimum.

And how could I have avoided adding a piece from that newspaper genius, Don Marquis, who fished in the hereafter with those anglers three: Noah an' Jonah an' Cap'n John Smith?

As with every collection, I suppose, it was with great regret that I had to cut and keep cutting. But perhaps these excerpts will excite and provoke the angler into finding the whole books for his winter angling and will sharpen his tranquil reflections of trout rising to the first May hatch on a sparkling day in spring.

Sausalito, California   EUGENE BURNS

I SHALL STAY HIM no longer than to wish him a rainy evening to read this following discourse; and that if he be an honest angler, the east wind may never blow when he goes a fishing.

Izaak Walton: THE COMPLEAT ANGLER, 1653.

The Angler

ENVY

I ENVY NOT HIM that eats better meat than I do; nor him that is richer, or that wears better clothes than I do: I envy him, and him only, that catches more fish than I do.

And such a man is like to prove an angler; and this noble emulation I wish to you, and all young anglers.

Izaak Walton: THE COMPLEAT ANGLER, 1653.

A WORM AT ONE END AND A FOOL AT THE OTHER

FLY-FISHING MAY BE a very pleasant amusement; but angling, or float-fishing, I can only compare to a stick and a string, with a *worm* at one end and a *fool* at the other.

Dr. Samuel Johnson: 1709-1784.

1

WHO IS, AND WHO IS NOT, AN ANGLER

ALMOST EVERYONE is now-a-days a *"piscator."* The *Fanatico,* about Easter, goes off as busy as the cockney on his *n*unter, when bound to Epping. He generally takes a great many things, and kills a few fish. Some dark, warm, windy, drizzly days, early or late in the season, and particularly when a fine breeze blows from off the banks of a river, where no one has begun fishing, the trout are so easily taken, that a basket full is but little proof of skill. One might then almost train a monkey to catch a trout. But, at other times, and particularly when fish are well fed, is the time to see who is, and who is not, an angler. About ninety in a hundred fancy themselves anglers. About one in a hundred *is* an angler. About ten in a hundred throw the hatchet better than the fly.

Col. Peter Hawker: INSTRUCTIONS TO YOUNG SPORTSMEN, 1814.

AND LYK A FISSHER

And lyk a fissher, as men alday may see,
  Baiteth his angle-hook with som pleasaunce,
'Til mony a fish is wook til that he be
Sesed ther-with; and then at erst hath he
  Al his desyr, and ther-with al michance;
  And thogh the lyne breke, he hath penaunce;
For with the hoke he wounded is so sore,
That he his wages hath for ever-more.

Geoffrey Chaucer: 1340-1400. THE COMPLEYNT OF MARS.

A VETERAN ANGLER

IN A MORNING'S STROLL along the banks of the Alun, a beautiful little stream which flows down from the Welsh hills and throws itself into the Dee, my attention was attracted to a group seated on the margin. On approaching, I found it to consist of a veteran angler and two rustic disciples. The former was an old fellow with a wooden leg, with clothes very

2

much but very carefully patched, betokening poverty honestly come by and decently maintained. His face bore the marks of former storms, but present fair weather; its furrows had been worn into an habitual smile; his iron-grey locks hung about his ears, and he had altogether the good-humored air of a constitutional philosopher who was disposed to take the world as it went. One of his companions was a ragged wight, with the skulking look of an arrant poacher, and I'll warrant could find his way to any gentleman's fish-pond in the neighborhood in the darkest night. The other was a tall, awkward country lad, with a lounging gait, and apparently somewhat of a rustic beau.

The old man was busy in examining the maw of a trout which he had just killed, to discover by its contents what insects were seasonable for bait; and was lecturing on the subject to his companions, who appeared to listen with infinite deference.

I have a kind feeling towards all "brothers of the angle," ever since I read Izaak Walton. They are men, he affirms, of a "mild, sweet, and peaceable spirit;" and my esteem for them has been increased since I met an old "Treatyse of Fysshynge Wyth An Angle," in which are set forth many of the maxims of their inoffensive fraternity. "Take good hede," sayeth this honest little treatyse, "that in going about your disportes ye open no man's gates but that ye shet them again. Also ye shall not use this forsyd crafti disport for no covetousness to the encrasing and sparing of your money only, but principally for your solace, and to cause the helth of your body and specyally of your soule."

I thought that I could perceive in the veteran angler before me an ex-emplification of what I had read; and there was a cheerful contentedness in his looks that quite drew me towards him. I could not but remark the gallant manner in which he stumped from one part of the brook to another; waving his rod in the air, to keep the line from dragging on the ground, or catching among the bushes; and the adroitness with which he would throw his fly to any particular place; sometimes skimming it lightly along a little rapid; sometimes casting it into one of those dark holes made by a twisted root or overhanging bank, in which the large trout are apt to lurk. In the meanwhile he was giving instructions to his two disciples; showing them the manner in which they should handle their rods, fix their flies, and play them along the surface of the stream.

The scene brought to my mind the instructions of the sage Piscator to his scholar. The country around was of that pastoral kind which Walton is fond of describing. It was a part of the great plain of Cheshire, close by

the beautiful vale of Gessford, and just where the inferior Welsh hills begin
to swell up from among fresh-smelling meadows. The day, too, like that
recorded in his work, was mild and sunshiny, with now and then a soft
dropping shower, that sowed the earth with diamonds.

Washington Irving: THE SKETCH BOOK, 1820.

THE CONTENTED ANGLER

The Angler hath a jolly life
  Who by the rail runs down,
And leaves his business and his wife,
  And all the din of town.
The wind downstream is blowing straight,
  And nowhere cast can he:
Then lo, he doth but sit and wait
  In kindly company.

Andrew Lang: 1844-1912.
Longmans Green & Co., Ltd.)

DANIEL WEBSTER'S MIGHTY STRONG TALK

OLD JOHN ATTAQUIN, then a patriarch among the few survivors of
the Mashpee Indians, had often been Mr. (Daniel) Webster's guide and
companion on his fishing trips and remembered clearly many of their hap-
penings. It was with a glow of love and admiration amounting almost to
worship that he related how this great fisherman, after landing a large trout
on the bank of the stream, "talked mighty strong and fine to that fish and
told him what a mistake he had made, and what a fool he was to take that
fly, and that he would have been all right if he had let it alone."

Who can doubt that patient search would disclose, somewhere in Mr.
Webster's speeches and writing, the elaboration, with high intent, of that
"mighty strong and fine" talk addressed to the fish at Mashpee?

Grover Cleveland: FISHING AND SHOOTING SKETCHES, 1906.
(The Macmillan Co., N. Y.)

CULTIVATE YOUR LUCK

FOR SOME MEN I admit the usefulness of skill and pertinacity; for myself, I take my stand entirely on luck. To the novice I would say: Cultivate your luck. Prop it up with omens and signs of good purport. Watch for magpies on your path. Form the habit of avoiding old women who squint. Throw salt over your left shoulder. Touch wood with the forefinger of your right hand whenever you are not doing anything else. Be on friendly terms with a black cat. Turn your money under the new moon. Walk round ladders. Don't start on a Friday. Stir the materials for Christmas pudding and wish. Perform all other such rites as you know or hear of.

Hugh T. Sheringham: COARSE FISHING, 1912.
(A. & C. Black, Ltd.)

CRUEL COXCOMB

And angling, too, that solitary vice,
Whatever Izaak Walton sings or says:
The quaint, old, cruel coxcomb, in his gullet
Should have a hook, & a small trout to pull it.

Lord Byron: DON JUAN (1819-1824).

PATIENCE, INDEED!

I SAY THEN, and will maintain it, that a salmon fisher should be strong in the arms, or he will never be able to keep on thrashing for ten or twelve hours together with a rod eighteen or twenty feet long, with ever and anon a lusty salmon at the end of his line, pulling like a wild horse with the lasso about him. Now he is obliged to keep his arms aloft, that the line may clear the rocks; now he must rush into the river, then back out with nimble pastern, always keeping his self-possession, "even in the very tempest and whirlwind of the sport," when the salmon rushes like a rocket. This is not moody work; it keeps a man alive and stirring. Patience, indeed!

William Scrope: DAYS AND NIGHTS OF SALMON-FISHING, 1843.
(James Blackwood & Co., Ltd.)

PROUD EPICUREAN BELLY-GODS

THE FISH was forty-five inches long, taken at Newberry in Barkshire, in England, with a casting net, a little after the Restoration of King Charles II by some citizens of London who came to that town to make merry with their Chapmen living there, and had been presented by the Mayor thereof to his said Majesty, as a Rairty, had not those Proud Epicurean Belly-gods been more intent in sacrificing to their own Net, and gratifying their covetous, greedy Appetites, than in paying a dutiful Reverence to their Sovereign.

Robert Howlett: THE ANGLER'S SURE GUIDE, 1706.

UTTER PERVERSITY

ONE DAY IN FALL I woke up and looked out the window at the first peep of dawn to find it a heavy, lowering morning with the clouds almost down to the ground; it seemed ready to rain any moment, but somehow I had the feeling that it wouldn't. In other words, it was the most ideal bass morning imaginable. I slipped out of bed and got a hasty breakfast.

A little while later found me a mile or so off, by boat drifting along the shoreline before a gentle breeze. I was being extremely careful to keep my casts at least six feet out from the edge of the bushes, or I should certainly have connected with a large bass, which might have ruined my temper and my day's fishing.

That may sound pretty silly, but if the experienced and foxy angler will think a moment, he'll probably chuckle; he'll have done the same thing himself. I was being watched, and I was afraid that if my observer knew I was catching fish he'd immediately start tossing a many-hooked plug uncomfortably close to my ears, while at the best he'd put the bass down so that they wouldn't strike again for a long time.

Presently the young man in the other boat called to ask how they were hitting. I pulled a long face and shook my head. "Whyyy So-so." Which can mean anything. Still, being by nature a friendly sort of chap, I wanted to help him to some sport if I could do it without having him ruin mine, so I asked him if he knew the lake hereabouts.

"Sure! I live in that house down there a hundred yards. But I haven't fished here in a couple of years; I've been away, where there was no fishing."

No fishing! And the man was polite, even pleasant, after two years of stark tragedy. He had fished a lot too, and he was a real sportsman; he was keeping far enough off not to scare any fish that might be near me.

"I got these," I said, and I pulled up my stringer. Generally, I liberate about all the fish I get, but we were having friends out to dinner and I wanted some for them.

His mouth flew open, and got stuck that way. At last he managed to gasp, "WH-where did you get 'em?"

"Right along here."

"And they're running that big!"

"Oh, no—I've kept only the biggest."

He seemed dazed. That string of huge bass was, obviously, a damn lie— the kind of lie we fishermen are accused of telling. But there it was He was silent a moment; maybe he was trying to decide whether he was still back in bed, dreaming.

"But, listen! I looked out the window only half an hour ago, and you weren't here."

"No—got 'em since."

He shook his head, looking at me in awe. "Do you always get 'em that way?"

That I certainly didn't, as I assured him. This was the finest morning for big bass I'd seen in at least a year; they seemed to have gone crazy, to be attempting mass suicide. But he—as I had noticed—hadn't been getting a single strike. He asked me deferentially if I'd show him how I did it. I told him to watch.

There were two trees growing out from the shore, about fifty feet from my boat. Since the lake was unusually high, their lower branches were in the water. They made a pocket about eight feet in diameter, with a sort of little gateway two feet or so across facing me. I sent my plug through that opening, let it rest several seconds, and then started it toward me just fast enough to keep it barely under water.

It had not gone a foot when it stopped gently, as though it had hung on an underwater twig. That was how the bass were taking that morning; they seemed torpid, lazy—until they found they were hooked, when they went wild. They acted as if they had been over-eating and it took a good jar to wake them up.

The fish landed and released, I looked around. Almost a hundred feet down the shore was another particularly promising pocket. Normally I'd have made perhaps a dozen casts before reaching it, but now I tossed my plug that way, watching to stop it in the air if I missed the opening—which, at that distance, was more likely than not. It chanced to go straight, and within five seconds I was battling another bass, a particularly rambunctious four-pounder.

I made two more casts, one a dud, the other picking up a very nice one. Three good bass in four casts—not bad, considering that this lake was within ten miles of downtown in one of our largest cities, and supposedly fished out two generations ago.

The last one released, I rowed over to the other man's boat to see how he was equipped. He had quite a good outfit, and there was a pike-scale plug on his leader—that usually worked well around here, as he probably had found out from former experience. But this particular morning they wanted no dealings with pike-scale plugs, for some reason known only to themselves. They wanted a red-head, and as he had one along I advised him to put it on. I asked if he could cast into the pockets without tangling up. "Lord no! I'd be hooked in the branches every time!"

"Then," I said, "cast as close to the bushes as you can; watch your plug and stop it in the air if it's going too far. But remember: this morning they just won't come out more than three feet after it; and if it's moving much faster than mine was, they won't bother with it at all. You won't get as many as in the pockets, but you'll get plenty of good ones within half an hour."

I advised him to begin at a big tree down the shore, where I'd started, and fish the other way. He headed back there while I kept on.

Presently I glanced around to see how he was doing. I got an object lesson in the sheer, utter perversity of human nature.

He was staying well out from the shore as he'd been doing before, and not putting his casts within fifteen feet of the bushes. And as soon as his plug struck the water, he'd start reeling back about as fast as he could. He'd begun at the big tree, all right—but he was following me along where I'd probably caught every fish, where those I'd released certainly wouldn't strike again so soon.

A suspicion came to me. I casually dropped back close enough to see what plug he was using. Yes—blamed if he didn't have his old reliable pike-scale back on again! Like all too many anglers, he had his favorite plug, type of water and retrieve, and he was sticking loyally to them, come hell or high water—or an empty stringer.

Jason Lucas: LUCAS ON BASS FISHING, 1947.
(Dodd, Mead & Co. Inc., N. Y.)

8

FIRST AT THE STREAM

YOU MIGHT SUPPOSE that the persons steathily emerging from the hotel at the break of day had been guilty of something, the discovery of which they are desirous to avoid. They are merely anxious, let us say, not to interfere with the slumbers of their brother anglers—of course from the purest motives of humanity.

The first grey of dawn still lingers over the valley and upon the hillsides when the first angler appears cautiously on the lawn. He glances around and notes with satisfaction that he is not forestalled, and that the wind blows down stream, and comes therefore from that quarter so dear to sportsmen.

The lithe rod is put together in a twinkling, the cast already prepared is affixed to the line, and the sharp whirr of the revolving winch wakes up the birds which densely populate the neighbourhood.

Soon other devotees of the gentle art arrive, and finding that they have not been able to lead off the operations of the day, as they had last night so resolutely determined, good-humoredly swallow their disappointment and fall-to with their weapons. But the fortunate gentleman down the lawn has not been twenty minutes at work before he has brought three trout to bank, and, like a sensible man and a knowing angler, hastens on to the lower meadow, to follow up his advantage.

William Senior: BY STREAM AND SEA, 1877.

THE MOTIONLESS ANGLER

Twilight leaned mirrored in a pool
Where willow boughs swept green and hoar,
Silk-clear the water, calm and cool,
Silent the woody shore:

There in abstracted, brooding mood
One fishing sate. His painted float
Motionless as a planet stood;
Motionless his boat.

Walter De la Mare: THE VEIL, 1873—.
(Henry Holt & Co. Inc.)

9

THEORIES: BY THE HOUR

TROUT, AS EVERYONE KNOWS who is an angler, never rise after a rain, nor before one; it is impossible to get them to rise in the heat; and any chill in the air keeps them down. The absolutely right day is a still, cloudy day, but even then there are certain kinds of clouds that prevent a rising of the trout. Indeed, I have only to say to one of my expert friends, "Queer, they didn't bite!" and he's off to a good start with an explanation. There is such a tremendous lot to know about trout fishing that men who are keen on it can discuss theories of fishing by the hour.

Stephen Leacock: HERE ARE MY LECTURES, 1936.
(Dodd, Mead & Co., Inc., N. Y.)

THE INWARD QUALITIES

NOW FOR THE INWARD QUALITIES of the minde, albeit some Writers reduce them into twelve heads, which indeed whosoever injoyeth cannot chuse but be very compleat in much perfection, yet I must draw them into many more Branches.

The First, and most especiall whereof, is, that a skilfull Angler ought to bee a generall Scholler, and seene in all the Liberall Sciences, as a Gramarian, to know how either to Write or Discourse of his Art in true and fitting termes, either without affectation or rudeness. Hee should have sweetnes of speech to perswade and intice other to delight in an Exercise so much Laudable. Hee should have strength of arguments to defend and maintane his profession, against Envy or slaunder.

Hee should have knowledge in the Sunne, Moone, and Starres, that by their Aspects hee may guesse the seasonablenesse, or unseasonablenesse of the weather, the breeding of stormes, and from what coasts the Windes are ever delivered.

Hee should bee a good knower of Countries, and well used to high wayes, that by taking the readiest pathes to every Lake, Brooke, or River, his journies may be more certaine, and lesse wearisome. Hee should have knowledge in proportions of all sorts, whether Circular, Square, or, Diametricall, that when hee shall be questioned of his diurnall progresses, hee may give a Geographicall description of the Angles and Channels of Rivers, how they fall from their heads, and what compasses they fetch in their severall windings.

Hee must also have the perfect Art of numbring, that in the soundings of Lakes or Rivers, hee may know how many foot or inches each severally contayneth, and by adding, subtracting, or multiplying the same, hee may yeeld the reason of every Rivers swift or slow Current.

Hee should not be unskillful in Musicke, that whensoever either melancholly, heavinesse of his thought, or the perturbations of his owne fancies stirreth up sadnesse in him, hee may remove the same with some godly Hymne or Antheme, of which David gives him ample examples.

Hee must be of a well setled and constant beliefe, to injoy the benefit of his Expectation, for then to Dispayre, it were better never to put in practise: And hee must ever thinke where the waters are pleasant and any thing likely, that there the Crator of all good things hath stored up much of his plenty: and though your satisfaction be not as ready as your wishes, yet you must hope still, that with perseverance you shall reap the fulnesse of your Harvest with contentment.

Then hee must be full of love, both to his pleasure and to his Neighbor; To his pleasure, which otherwise would be irkesome and tedious, and to his neighbor that he neither give offence in any particular, nor be guilty of any generall distruction.

Then he must be exceeding patient, and neither vexe or excruciate himselfe with losses or mischances, as in losing the prey when it is almost in the hand, or by breaking his Tooles by ignorance or negligence, but with a pleased sufferance amend his errors, and thinke mischances instructions to better carefullnesse.

He must then be full of humble thoughts, not disdayning when occasion commands to kneele, lye downe, or wet his feet or fingers, as oft as there is any advantage given thereby, unto the gaining the end of his labour.

Then he must be strong and valiant, neither to be amazed with stormes, nor affrighted with thunder, but to hold them according to their naturall causes, and the pleasure of the Highest: neither must he, like the Foxe, which preyeth upon Lambes, imploy all his labour against a smaller frie, but like the Lyon that feazeth Elephants, thinke the greatest Fish which swimmeth, a reward lille enough for the paines which he endureith.

Then must he be liberall, and not working onely for his owne belly, as if it could never be satisfied; but he must with much cheerfulnesse bestow the fruites of his skill amongst his honest neighbours, who being partners of his game, will doubly renown his tryumph, and that is ever pleasing reward to vertue.

Then he musst be prudent, that apprehending the Reasons why the Fish will note bite, and all other casuall impediments which hinder his sport, and knowing the Remedies for them same, hee may direct his Labours to be without trouble fommesse: Then hee must have a moderate contention of the mind, to be satisfied with indifferent things, and not out of an avaricious greedinesse thinke every thing too little, be it never so abundant.

Then must he be of a thankefull nature, praising the Author of all goodnesse, and shewing a large gratefulnesse for the least satisfaction.

Then must he bee of a perfect memory, quicke, and prompt to call into his mind all the needful things which are any way in his Exercise to be imployed, lest by omission or by forgetfulnesse of any, he frustrate his hopes, and make his Labour effectlesse.

Lastly, he must be of a strong constitution of body, able to endure much fasting, and not of a gnawing stromacke, observing houres, in which if it be unsatisfied, it troubleth both the mind and body, and loseth that delight which maketh the pastime onely pleasing.

Gervase Markham: (1568-1637): COUNTRY CONTENTMENTS.

THE FISHER

TEACHER: What craft do you know?
PUPIL: I am a fisherman.

TEACHER: What do you get from your craft?
PUPIL: Food, and clothes, and money.

TEACHER: How do you catch fish?
PUPIL: I go aboard my ship, and cast my net into the water, and throw out my hook, and my basket, and whatever they capture I take.

TEACHER: What if the fish are unclean?
PUPIL: I throw the unclean out and take the clean ones for food.

TEACHER: Where do you sell your fish?
PUPIL: In the city.

TEACHER: Who buys them?

PUPIL: The people in the city. I am not able to take as many as I am able to sell.

TEACHER: What kind of fish do you catch?

PUPIL: Eeles, and Haddocks, Menows, Ale-Pout, Trout, and Lamprey, and whatever fish swim in the water.

TEACHER: Why don't you fish in the sea?

PUPIL: Sometimes I do, but not often, because I have to row a good deal to get to the sea.

TEACHER: What do you catch on the sea?

PUPIL: Herrings, Salmon, Porpoise, Sturgeon, Oysters, Crabs, Muscles, Shell-fish, Cockles, Lobsters, and many such.

TEACHER: Will you catch a whale?

PUPIL: No.

TEACHER: Why not?

PUPIL: Because it is a dangerous thing to catch a whale. It is safer for me to go out on the river with my ship than to go with my ship to hunt whales.

TEACHER: Why so?

PUPIL: Because I prefer to take fish that I am able to destroy, than a fish that may sink or kill me and likewise my companions with one lick!

TEACHER: And nevertheless many do catch whales and they escape danger, and make a great deal of money at it.

PUPIL: You are telling the truth but I do not dare to on account of the want of enterprise of my disposition.

Archbishop Aelfric, COLLOQUY No. 53., *Roughly, 1000 A.D.*
(Oldest reference to fishing written in English)

The Boy

MY FIRST TROUT

As I APPROACHED my tenth year I became more and more devoted to my fishing-rod, and with a little knot of friends as enthusiastic as myself, I used to pass every hour unclaimed by our schoolmaster in spinning hair-lines, making tackle and bobbing for eels.

On one of our holiday afternoons the little party of friends repaired to the Browney, near Langley Bridge, and there in the long Dub by the side of the Brancepeth road we propped our rods side by side and began a game at leap-frog, when a cry arose, "There's a bite at Henderson's." A rush to the river, an anxious pause, a gentle uplifting of the rod, a loud scream of wonder and backwards I ran, far into the dusty road, dragging a trout whose weight was at least a pound.

The war-whoops and dances of a party of Indians could hardly have exceeded the excitement to which we gave way. There was cheer upon cheer, yell upon yell, and many a thump descended upon my back. There was no more fishing that afternoon. Back we marched to the old city, bearing our prize suspended by the gills upon a hazel stick and looking out for the admiring gaze of the passers-by. The Iron Duke, when Waterloo had been fought and won, was not more proud than we.

William Henderson: MY LIFE AS AN ANGLER, 1879.

A BOY LOVES TO PLAY

Where the pools are bright and deep,
Where the grey trout lies asleep,
Up the river and o'er the lea,
That's the way for Billy and me.

Where the blackbird sings the latest,
Where the hawthorn blooms the sweetest,
Where the nestlings chirp and flee,
That's the way for Billy and me.

Where the mowers mow the cleanest,
Where the hay lies thick and greenest,
There to track the homeward bee,
That's the way for Billy and me.

Where the hazel bank is steepest,
Where the shadow falls the deepest,
Where the clustering nuts fall free,
That's the way for Billy and me.

Why the boys should drive away
Little sweet maidens from the play,
Or love to banter and fight so well,
That's the thing I never could tell.

But this I know, I love to play
Through the meadow, among the hay,
Up the water and o'er the lea,
That's the way for Billy and me.

James Hogg, 1770-1835.

THE COUNTRY LAD

Who can live in heart so glad
As the merry country lad?
Who upon a fair green balk
May at pleasure sit and walk,
And amid the azure skies
See the morning sun arise,
While he hears in every spring
How the birds do chirp and sing:
Or before the hounds in cry
See the hare go stealing by:
Or along the shallow brook
Angling with a baited hook,
See the fishes leap and play
In a blessed sunny day:
Or to hear the partridge call,
Till she have her covey all:
Or to see the subtle fox
How the villain plies the box:
After feeding on his prey
How he closely sneaks away
Through the hedge and down the furrow
Till he gets into his burrow:
Then the bee to gather honey,
And the little black-haired coney,
On a bank for sunny place,
With her forefeet wash her face:
Are not these with thousands moe
Than the courts of kings do know,
The true pleasing spirit's sights
That may breed true love's delights?

Nicholas Breton, 1604. THE PASSIONATE SHEPHEARD.

TO TOM HUGHES

Come away with me, Tom,
Term and talk are done;
My poor lads are reaping,
Busy every one.
Curates mind the parish,
Sweepers mind the court;
We'll away to Snowdon
For our ten days' sport;
Fish the August evening
Till the eve is past,
Whoop like boys, at pounders
Fairly played and grassed.
When they cease to dimple,
Lunge, and swerve, and leap,
Then up over Siabod,
Choose our nest, and sleep.
Up a thousand feet, Tom,
Round the lion's head,
Find soft stones to leeward
And make up our bed.
Eat our bread and bacon,
Smoke the pipe of peace,
And, ere we be drowsy,
Give our boots a grease.
Homer's heroes did so,
Why not such as we?
What are sheets and servants?
Superfluity!

Charles Kingsley: THE INVITATION, 1856.

TOM BROWN AND VELVETEENS

Now CAME ON the may-fly season; the soft hazy summer weather lay sleepily along the rich meadows by Avon side, and the green and grey flies flickered with their graceful lazy up and down flight over the reeds and the water and the meadows, in myriads upon myriads. The may-flies must surely be the lotus-eaters of the ephemerae; the happiest, laziest, carelessest fly that dances and dreams out his few hours of sunshiny life by English river.

So, one fine Thursday afternoon, Tom, having borrowed East's new rod, started by himself to the river. He fished for some time with small success, not a fish would rise at him; but, as he prowled along the bank, he was presently aware of mighty ones feeding in a pool on the opposite side, under the shade of a huge willow tree. The stream was deep here, but some fifty yards below was a shallow, for which he made off hot-foot; and forgetting landlords, keepers, solemn prohibitions of the doctor, and everything else, pulled up his trousers, plunged across, and in three minutes was creeping along on all fours towards the clump of willows.

It isn't often that great chub, or any other coarse fish, are in earnest about anything, but just then they were thoroughly bent on feeding, and in half-an-hour Master Tom had deposited three thumping fellows at the foot of the giant willow. As he was baiting for a fourth pounder, and just going to throw in again, he became aware of a man coming up the bank not one hundred yards off. Another look told him that it was the under-keeper. Could he reach the shallow before him? No, not carrying his rod. Nothing for it but the tree; so Tom laid his bones to it, shinning up as fast he could, and dragging up his rod after him.

He had just time to reach and crouch along upon a huge branch some ten feet up, which stretched out over the river, when the keeper arrived at the clump. Tom's heart beat fast as he came under the tree; two steps more and he would have passed, when, as ill-luck would have it, the gleam on the scales of the dead fish caught his eye, and he made a dead point at the foot of the tree. He picked up the fish one by one; his eye and touch told him that they had been alive and feeding within the hour.

Tom crouched lower along the branch, and heard the keeper beating the clump. "If I could only get the rod hidden," thought he, and began gently shifting it to get it alongside him; "willow trees don't throw out straight hickory shoots twelve feet long, with no leaves, worse luck." Alas! the keeper catches the rustle, and then a sight of the rod, and then of Tom's hand and arm.

19

"Oh, be up ther', be 'ee?" says he, running under the tree. "Now you come down this minute."

"Tree'd at last," thinks Tom, making no answer, and keeping as close as possible, but working away at the rod, which he takes to pieces. "I'm in for it, unless I can starve him out." And then he begins to meditate getting along the branch for a plunge, and a scramble to the other side; but the small branches are so thick, and the opposite bank so difficult, that the keeper will have lots of time to get round by the ford before he can get out, so he gives that up. And now he hears the keeper beginning to scramble up the trunk. That will never do; so he scrambles himself back to where his branch joins the trunk, and stands with lifted rod.

"Hullo, Velveteens, mind your fingers if you come any higher."

The keeper stops and looks up, and then with a grin says, "Oh, be you, be it, young measter? Well, here's luck. Now I tells 'ee to come down at once, and 't'll be best for 'ee."

"Thank 'ee, Velveteens, I'm very comfortable," said Tom, shortening the rod in his hand, and preparing for battle.

"Werry well, please yourself," said the keeper descending, however, to the ground again, and taking his seat on the bank; "I bean't in no hurry, so you med take your time. I'll larn 'ee to gee honest folk names afore I've done with 'ee."

"My luck as usual," thinks Tom; "what a fool I was to give him a black. If I'd called him 'keeper' now I might get off. The return match is all his way."

The keeper quietly proceeded to take out his pipe, fill, and light it, keeping an eye on Tom, who now sat disconsolately across the branch, looking at keeper—a pitiful sight for men and fishes. The more he thought of it the less he liked it. "It must be getting near second calling-over," thinks he. Keeper smokes on stolidly. "If he takes me up. I shall be flogged safe enough. I can't sit here all night. Wonder if he'll rise at silver."

"I say, keeper," said he meekly, "let me go for two bob?"

"Not for twenty neither," grunts his persecutor.

And so they sat on till long past second calling-over, and the sun came slanting in through the willow-branches, and telling of locking-up near at hand.

"I'm coming down, keeper," said Tom at last with a sigh, fairly tired out. "Now what are you going to do?"

"Walk 'ee up to School, and give 'ee over to the Doctor, them's my orders," says Velveteens, knocking the ashes out of his fourth pipe, and standing up and shaking himself.

"Very good," said Tom; "but hands off, you know. I'll go with you quietly, so no collaring or that sort of thing."

Keeper looked at him a minute. "Werry good," said he at last; and so Tom descended and wended his way drearily by the side of the keeper up to the School-house, where they arrived just at locking-up. As they passed the School gates, the Tadpole and several others who were standing there caught the state of things, and rushed out, crying "Rescue!" but Tom shook his head, so they only followed to the Doctor's gate and went back sorely puzzled.

How changed and stern the Doctor seemed from the last time that Tom was up there, as the keeper told the story, not omitting to state Tom had called him blackguard names. "Indeed, sir," broke in the culprit, "it was only Velveteens."

The Doctor only asked one question, "You know the rule about the banks, Brown?"

"Yes, sir."

"Then wait for me to-morrow after first lesson."

"I thought so," muttered Tom.

Thomas Hughes: TOM BROWN'S SCHOOLDAYS, 1857.
(The Macmillan Co.)

COME ALONG TO THE SQUIRE

WITHIN THE BORDERS of Brookhaven Township, rich in sporting lore, I came upon a little brook whose denizens were eating lunch in a most tantalizing manner. It took but a minute to cut a switch, rig a March Brown to my line, and descend the bank to within casting distance. By means of certain methods known to brook fishers I managed to put my fly first over this trout and then over that one. In half an hour there were five fish lying in the ferns behind me.

Utterly oblivious to my surroundings, I was about to make the number six, when a voice with a soft South Bay drawl asked me where in hell I thought I was?

I almost answered heaven, but caught myself in time to stammer that I didn't know—exactly.

I was then informed by the owner of the voice that I had better come along and see the "squire;" mebbe he'd tell me. Further palaver brought out the fact that I was inadvertently poaching on the property of a club, and that the voice belonged to the watchman whose duty it was to apprehend such miscreants as myself. My trout—I maintain that the ownership of the trout is vested in him who can catch them, especially from a small brook,—were pocketed for evidence, and we were about to start out to make the squire's acquaintance, when a hearty-looking old gentleman came upon the scene.

After greeting the watchman the newcomer must have divined my plight, for he hemmed and hawed a bit before inquiring about the fishing. I told him that the trout had been taking a March Brown nicely, and that the watchman had a sample of them in his pocket. At that the old gentleman swung around on my captor with fire in his eye. The watchman looked uncomfortable and surprised under the lowering gaze which was directed at him.

"Jim, have you robbed the young gentleman of his trout?"

"No sir, I ain't! I caught this feller poachin' here, an' I'm going' to fetch him to the squire."

"POACHING! Hellity demmit, sir! A guest of mine *poaching?* Apologize to the young gentleman, sir, and take yourself out of my sight!"

As soon as Jim had removed his obnoxious presence from the scene, my rescuer turned to me with a twinkle in his eye, and chuckled, and said that he was delighted that I had been able to accept his invitation to fish the brook! and would I honor him by coming to the house for lunch where we could test the quality of my catch on the table.

Eugene V. Connett, 3rd, ANY LUCK, 1933.
Windward House, Publishers.

The Fish

THE PRINCELY TROUT

THE TROUT in his prime is a princely fish; he hath his teeth in his moouth; is of courage bold, of great agility, quickness of sight, and very wary too. His outward form is comely, his complexions various. Bespangled with delicate spots of dark and red, and to eat hath a delightful taste.

Robert Howlett: THE ANGLER'S SURE GUIDE, 1706.

THE KING OF FISH

OF THE SALMON: He's the largest of fresh Water fish, and therefore, as well as for the super-excellency of his Nature, is called the King of fresh Water Fish. He's a fish of prey, has his teeth in his Mouth, and when in Season is very beautiful, being adorned with a Row of small, round, black Spots, all along the middle of each side, from Head to Tail.

His Flesh is wonderful sweet, and of extraordinary Nourishment, and therefore, unless eaten moderately, causeth Surfeits, is restorative in Consumprions, and if pickled like Sturgeons, strengthens the Stomach much, and provockes an Appetite.

Our Thames, Severn, and the worthy River Ex, are in vogue for the best Salmon in England, of incomparable relish, and pleasant taste, and are as good as any be in any part of the world, by the Opinion of Geographers, not by Reason of the Prosimity of these Rivers to the Sea, ebbing and flowing so far up them; but because of their Largeness, Commodiousness, Swiftness, Stony and Gravelly Soil, which makes their Waters so pure and clear and Christaline, and of so Slubrious and Nutritious a Nature.

Anonymous

THE WAY OF FISHES GENERATING

CONCERNING THE GENERATING of Fishes, philosophy doth hold, that those which are the same kind, couple not, nor perform any Act of Generation with any other Fish of a different species, as Carps with Breams, etc.

The way of Fishes generating is various.

Of Salmons, trouts, carps, etc, by the Females shedding the Spawn in places convenient, and the Milter's casting his Sperm upon it; in which the Animal Spirit abideth, till sooner or later the young are brought forth; for the Spirit may be bound in its Seed with the Cold, so as that for a time, it cannot exercise its Operation; for, as grains of corn kept all winter in the earth, do bud nevertheless; So the Eggs of Fishes scatter'd in an apt matter, receive not Formation till the generative Heat of the Sun hath sufficient Influence upon them.

Of silver eels by coupling or joyning together, no not much unlike to Dewworms.

Of some fish by gliding their bellies one against the other with that Clerity, that humane eyes can scarce perceive it.

When a spawner or female Carp goes to cast her Spawn, three or four milters, ie, Male carps follow her, and she dissembling a Coyness, they force her through weeds, flags, etc., where she lets fall her spawn, which sticks fast to the weeds, etc. Then the males come and shed their Milt upon it, and all the spawn that is touched with the milt of the males in a short time become living fish, and none else; and she being weakened by doing that natural office, the milters help her off from the shallows and weeds by bearing her up on both sides, and guarding her into the deeps.

Of others, by being gendred of Slime and Rottenness that is on the Water: And all these observe the kind: But say some, the Lamprey, which at the hissing of the Viper, comes onshaore and ingenders with it. Which, by the way, (if true) is an Argument that Fish do hear. And some other Philosophers affirm, that Adders be venimous both in Body and Sperm; but to salve this, they would have us believe, the Adder puts away his venom before he genders with the Lamprey, and after, takes it again; by which means the Lamprey participates not of the Serpent's poison: But I am of Forath's Opinion, *Lib. de Animalibus,* that the Lamprey genders only with its own kind, and not with any kind of Serpent.

Robert Howlett
The Angler's Sure Guide, 1706.

SALMONIDAE

TROUT AND SALMON are much alike. They are members of the family *Salmonidae.* Natives of the northern hemisphere only, they are spread through Europe, Asia, and North America. They have taken up their abode in Corsica and Sardinia and Switzerland, in the rushing torrents of the Pyrenees and the quiet brooks of Normandy, in the clear English chalk streams and the rough Welsh currents, in the smiling Loire and the majestic Rhine. They have entered the rivers of Scotland and Wales. They have made Restigouche and Beaverkill and Nipigon and Gunnison and Klamath great names in the American fisherman's geography. But they have never crossed the equator. If the New Zealander and the South African are able to share in their English cousins' piscatorial pastimes, it is only because the trout and the salmon have been transported by ship across warm equatorial waters which they have never penetrated under their own power.

Brian Curtis: THE LIFE STORY OF THE FISH, 1949.
(Harcourt, Brace & Co., New York).

KTAADN TROUT

THE TRUE TROUT took their turn and alternately the speckled trout, and the silvery roaches, swallowed the bait as fast as we could throw in; and the finest specimens of both that I have ever seen, the largest one weighing three pounds, were heaved upon the shore. While yet alive, before their tints had faded, they glistened like the fairest flowers, the product of primitive rivers; and he could hardly trust his senses, as he stood over them, that these jewels should have swam away in that Aboljacknagesic water for so long, so many dark ages;—these bright fluviatile flowers, seen of Indians only, made beautiful, the Lord only knows why, to swim there! I could understand better for this, the truth of mythology, the fables of Proteus, and all those beautiful sea-monsters,—how all history, indeed, put to a terrestrial use, is mere history; but put to a celestial, is mythology always.

But there is the rough voice of Uncle George, who commands at the frying pan, to send over what you've got, and then you may stay till morning. The pork sizzles and cries for fish. Luckily for the foolish race, and this particular foolish generation of trout, the night shut down at last, not a little deepened by the dark side of Ktaadn, which, like a permanent shadow, reared itself from the eastern bank.

In the night I dreamed of trout-fishing; and, when at length I awoke, it seemed a fable that this painted fish swam there so near my couch, and rose to our hooks the last evening, and I doubted if I had not dreamed it all. So I arose before dawn to test its truth, while my companions were still sleeping. There stood Ktaadn with distinct and cloudless outline in the moonlight; and the rippling of the rapids was the only sound to break the stillness. Standing on the shore, I once more cast my line into the stream, and found the dream to be real and the fable true.

Henry D. Thoreau, 1817-1862.

THE MELANCHOLY PIKE

THE PIKE is a melancholy fish, swims by himself, and lives alone. His flesh is very medicinal. His spawn and row provoke both to vomit and stool, and are used for that purpose; the jaws calcin'd helps the Stone, cleanses and dries up Ulcers, old Sores and Hemorrhoids; the Teeth in Poser gives Ease in the Pleurisei; the Grease takes away Coughs in Children, by anointing the Feet therewith; the Gall taken inwardly, cures the Agues; outwardly helps Spots and dimness of the Eyes; the Heart eaten cures Fevers.

Anonymous

THE FISH DESTROYER

AMONGST ALL THE RAVENOUR CREATURES which Destroy Fish there is
none more greedy than the Otter, whose only food being thereon, hourely
lyeth in waite to consume them: therefore though some Fisher-men use
to take him with a Weele made with a double tunnell, and called by the
name of the Otter-weele, whose practise is so ordinary that every Fisherman knows the use of the same; yet for a more ready and easie way to
destroy him, you shall as neere as you can find out his haunt, and holes
that are in the banke, and under the Roots of Trees where he lodgeth, and
then take a great Eele, and slitting her back above her navel, put in three
or four lumps of Arsnicke, and then stich up the skin againe, and so lay
the Eele from the navell downward in the water, and from the navell upward out of the water: which when the Otter finds, it is his property to
eate unto the navell and no further which if he do it is certaine that is the
last he will eate.

Gervase Markham (1568-1637): COUNTRY CONTENTMENTS.

THE SALMON IS TOO CUMBERSOME

Now, LASTLY, touching the angling for Salmon, albeit he is a fish which
in truth is unfit for your Travaile, both because hee is too huge and cumbersome, as also in that hee naturally delighteth to lie in the bottome of
great deepe Rivers, and as neere as may bee in the middlest of the Channell,
yet for as much as many men esteeme that best which is got with most
difficulty, you shall understand that the baites in which hee most delightest
are those which serve for the trout, as paste, or flyes in the Summer, and
Red-wormes, Bob-wormes, or Cankers on the water-dockes after Michaelmas.

Gervase Markham (1568-1637): COUNTRY CONTENTMENTS.

The Great Old Fish

FISHING IN CHILE

THERE IS A SCOT in Valpariso, the third generation of his family to be born in the country, who is reputed to be the best fly-fisherman in Chile. He came into my room in the hospital where I was lying, introduced himself, and said: "When you get out of here, I am going to give you some fishing that will take the hair off your head." So a few nights later he and I were in a train for southern Chile—for Chillan, the town which was literally wiped off the map by an earthquake a few years later. From Chillan we drove the next day, some forty or fifty miles, I think, to a little village between us and the far, blue, broken silhouette of the Andes: they lay like a jagged line of broken blue glass along the eastern sky.

The volcano of Chillan, on our left, was erupting every ten minutes. So regularly that you could set your watch by it, it shot a 2,000-foot feather of sulphur yellow into the blue sky every ten minutes. And three times when I had on my first fish I saw that feather shoot up.

This river was the Laja, racing down from the extinct volcano of Antuco in the far Andes. In the long flat sweeps it was a deep bottle-green . . . but

29

swirling. Then it crashed through the rocks it had rounded through the ages, poured white over the ledges, and emitted the continuous low roar of broken water. I remembered what the ambassador had told me in Santiago—"plenty of backing on your line"—and my heart sank.

At any rate, I told myself, put on the biggest leader you've got (it was a 2X), soak it well . . . and trust heaven. It was well I did.

I had picked the side of a broad stretch of white falls where the main river swept past in frothing white water and where there was a lee of green water lying along the main current. I felt that if there were any big trout, waiting for something to come down, this was where they would be. It was easy casting, for there was no high brush behind me, and I kept as long a line as I could in the air, hoping to reach the edge of the white water. I think I must have been even more shocked than the fish when, on my very first cast, just as my fly was sweeping down about opposite me, I got that driving pull of a heavy strike. It was the first cast I made in Chile—and it was the best fish.

Without waiting for any more argument he went straight on down the river, sweeping through the white water, where he seemed to rest, or sulk, for a moment in the green water on the other side. It was lucky for me that he did; practically every foot of my line had been taken out. So there we were. I could not get across to him. Neither could I get him across to me. So I gave him the bend of the rod while I stood there and thought about it.

In these parts of Chile there is a very poor brand of peasants, which exists heaven knows how; they come about as close to living without any visible means of support as you would think man could get. There was the brush-board-and-thatched hovel of one of these ramshackle humans behind me now. Its inhabitants had evidently been watching me for some time. Now, seeing me standing there, apparently doing nothing, a small urchin impelled by curiosity came cautiously up to see what I was doing. We spoke no language in which we could communicate with each other; and when I unhooked my landing-net and snapped it open he almost fainted from fright. But he was a quick-witted little fellow, and, somehow, he comprehended what a net was. I made him take it from me.

So there were two of us standing there now. The fish had remained exactly where he was. I gave him a slow pull. The next instant the fish was going down along his side of the river and the boy and I were stumbling down along the boulders on ours. As I said, these strange, volcanic rocks had been rounded by time, and a more tricky, stumbling, infuriating

30

river journey I have seldom made. For I was deep in the river by now, getting as close to the fish as I could get in order to win back some more line. In this fashion I took several yards back from him. Then I reached a high stretch of bank where the water was too deep, and so came back to land. It was now, I said gloomily to myself, that I would lose this fish; for, some fifty yards below me, shone a long sloping shelf of white water in the mid-day sun.

Then the fish took it into his head to command operations. To my confused delight and dismay he came directly at me across the white water, so fast that I could barely strip in the line, I had no chance to reel in. Then he went on up the river, taking the line with him as fast as I could pay it out without fouling it. Then, boring against the line, as if he meant to jump the low falls, he again remained stationary over one spot.

This was exactly what the doctor ordered. I could not have asked him to do anything nicer. Reeling in as swiftly as I could, I worked my way up to him. So there, plus one Chilean boy, we were exactly where we had started over twenty minutes before. I knew it was twenty minutes, because twice during our tussle, I had seen Chillan erupt. That 2,000-foot sulphurous jet!

Now began one of the most beautiful battles I have ever experienced. For I had plenty of line in hand now; when he came past I gave him the bend of the rod for all I thought it could stand—determined he should never cross to the other side of that white water again. And every time I checked him. The green water was so glass-clear that when he swung in the swirls sluicing past me the sun caught and reflected the pinkish stripe along his strong sides. I could watch him fighting the hook. And then he spun in the sun, jumping. He was the very essence of fight. Furious, I think —still not frightened.

There is no doubt that in the ingredients of a fisherman's delight there is nothing comparable to being able to watch a fish fight like this. For I could see him, or his shape, nearly all the time. Chillan erupted once more.

By now my gallant Rainbow was a slow-moving, sullen thing. His tail working heavily, he lay in the green water about twenty yards out from me. And I looked around for the lee of some rocks and slowly worked him in. I had him in a pool. It was almost still water. He was almost resting against the hook. And then, as the bank was high, and I was an idiot, I signalled the little Chilean boy to wade out and slip the net under him.

The boy did. He was an eager boy . . . so eager that he stabbed the net at the fish . . . pushed him with it! Then he tried to scoop him in from the tail . . . I jumped. As I did, the boy actually got the fish into the net. I seized boy, net, fish, all at the same time, and threw them all up on the bank. There I dived on my fish.

It all goes to prove the hysterical condition into which some fishermen will get themselves. For this Rainbow was not much over six pounds. But he was such a beautiful one! That was the point; that small nose, and those deep shoulders, and those firm fighting flanks. This fish had been living in clean water on crayfish galore. I sat on the bank and looked at him for nearly twenty minutes.

Then I went to fishing again.

Negley Farson: GOING FISHING, 1943.
(Harcourt, Brace & Co., New York).

LASHING TENTACLES

I WAS swimming home late one afternoon, face in the water and spear couched when I saw a bat-like shadow moving along below me. It was dark brown and a yard across. It swam with an undulating slither close to the bottom. Occasionally a portion of it would fold together, as a butcher might fold a piece of raw liver, and then the folded part became a long tapering tentacle which licked around the rocks like a whiplash in slow action. Even if I hadn't guessed what it was I'd have recognized an octopus soon enough, for suddenly it folded itself into eight distinct tenacles radiating from a central tumorous lump like a derby hat and looked up at me with a pair of protruding gold-rimmed eyes. Not knowing what else to do, I looked back at him through a pair of nickel-rimmed goggles. He didn't make a hostile move, and neither did I. I could see his head, which was also his body, pulsating in an oozy, intestinal sort of way, and as his tentacles writhed gently I caught glimpses of the rows of bony white suction cups along the under sides of them.

Italian fishermen had told me that if an octopus gets you when you are unarmed, the thing to do is bite him between the eyes, thus paralyzing the master nerve which controls his tentacles. Not caring to make the headlines by improving upon the old newspaper formula MAN BITES DOG, I swam down and jabbed him with the spear. I was nervous and my lunge went wild; I missed his eyes, but got him through the bulbous, palpitating body. Instantly the submarine day turned into darkest night, and I found myself being towed through a cloud of ink which he shot from his breathing apparatus as he pumped himself along. Once clear of the cloud, I saw that he was swimming with his tentacles streaming out behind him like the tail of a comet. He groped down, grabbed a rock and started climbing along the side of it toward a cave. If the five-pronged spear was hurting he didn't show it; all he registered was annoyance.

Well, I had to have air, but though I dragged with all my force, he dragged harder. I let go the spear, struggled up and breathed in air. I went under again. The octopus was out of sight now, but the spear handle was jutting from the cave. I grabbed it with both hands. I tried using it as a lever against the top of the cavern, but slowly it was dragged inward. Then, suddenly, a tentacle lashed out and wrapped itself around the wood, then another, and another. In his rage he was letting go of the rock and trying to strangle the spear. A fourth tentacle snaked out, caught the spear handle and licked across the back of my left hand. The part that touched me was only the tapering tip, but I didn't care for the nasty sucking feel of it. With a final tug I broke his hold on the rock, brought him to the surface and then ashore.

Guy Gilpatrick: THE COMPLEAT GOGGLER, 1938.
(Dodd, Mead & Co., Inc., New York).

DOLLYS FOR A BEAR

THE survey crew—Johnny and Ray and Frank and myself—had gone out to camp about four miles from Deer Creek (in Washington). Johnny and Frank were both quite newly married and liked to get back to Camp 7, the main camp, over each weekend; Ray generally went with them. That left me free to get away for Deer Creek sometime on Saturday afternoon and stay there until almost dark on Sunday night.

The first of these weekends was in many ways the best of them all, partly because the whole experience was new to me and partly because of the bears. Our camp, like Deer Creek itself, was some twelve or thirteen hundred feet above sea level, but the country immediately around it was a big flat which the bears seemed to like.

I came to Deer Creek at a fine pool above a log jam. The river was a lot bigger than the word "creek" had led me to expect, and it was beautiful, clear and bright and fast, tumbled on rocks and gravel bars. I was standing on a wide gravel bar which gave me every chance to cast and fish as I wished, and my heart beat hard and my fingers trembled as I dumped my pack and began to put my rod up—they do that even today when I come to the bank of a river I have not seen before and find the reality of it better than anything I had dared hope.

I had brought in with me a nine-foot casting rod, a Silex reel and a boxful of the spoons and devon minnows and phantoms we had used for salmon on the Dorsetshire Frome. As soon as the rod was up and the line was threaded, I went up to the head of the pool and began to fish. I made cast after cast, swinging the minnow across as slow and deep as I could. The pool became slower and deeper, and I really began to expect a fish. The minnow touched bottom several times among the big round rocks, and I knew I was deep enough. I made a cast whose swing carried the minnow almost under the log jam and felt a sharp, heavy strike. This was it, I told myself, a steelhead at last.

The fish ran almost instantly from the strike, and I held hard to turn him from the log jam. It was a strong run, clear across the river; then he came back a little, and I began to think of the stories. In spite of anything I could do, he would run again under the log jam and break me there. He ought to jump soon; all the stories said they jumped like mad things.

I began to walk him upstream, away from the jam, and at first he came quietly enough. Then he seemed to decide that he wanted to go that way anyhow, and he ran steadily and smoothy right up to the head of the pool.

Still there was no jumping and no sign of the fierce strength of a good fish that raps the handle of the reel against your knuckles and makes you think you really have lost control this time.

I put pressure on him, and he came into the shallow water at the foot of the gravel bar steadily, and quietly. I walked close and lifted him to the surface; he struggled and bored away once, came back and was finished, quiet on his side on top of the water. I ran him up on the beach without difficulty and stooped down to look him over. He was a fish of about four pounds, silver grey all over, very little darker on the back than on the belly; he was thick and fat, and along his sides there were pale lemon-colored spots.

I didn't think he was a steelhead. I almost hoped he wasn't, because he was so far from what I had looked forward to, in strength, size, fighting quality, beauty, everything. Yet no one had warned me to expect any other fish but steelhead in Deer Creek, and it was hard to believe that such a good-sized handsome fish, as this certainly was, could be overlooked. Doubtfully I went back to my fishing.

I caught three more fish that evening, all almost exactly like the first one. Not one of them had jumped; but all had fought well enough for their size, and at least they made something to take back to camp.

I went up from the creek a little before dark and made camp beside a small stream that ran down to it. After fifty feet below my camp the stream ran shallow under a big log, and I threw the fish down there, thinking it was cool and shaded and they would keep well through the heat of the next day. Then I made supper and rolled happily into my single blanket, tired, thoroughly contented, in love with Deer Creek and fully determined that it should show me a steelhead next day.

I woke in the quiet dim light before sunrise. For once I didn't want to go on sleeping. There was a whole day of Deer Creek ahead, and I sat straight up in my blanket. Below me, near the log where my fish were, I saw a movement. It was a bear, a fine, handsome black bear who hadn't the slightest idea I was within a hundred miles of him. For a moment I was more pleased than scared; then I realized he was eating my good Dolly Vardens, for that was what months later, I found they were. I yelled in fury. He looked up at me, and I thought he looked calm and contented, as he very well may have. I reached for my boots and yelled again, and he turned round then, lifting his forepaws from the ground in that lovely liquid movement bears have. I drew back a boot to throw at him—a logger's calked boot at fifty feet is something of a weapon—but he didn't wait for that. I pulled on my boots and went down to look at the wreck of my fish. His meal had not really been disturbed; my first yell had come merely as a grace at the end of it.

Roderick L. Haig-Brown, 1946. A RIVER NEVER SLEEPS.
(William Morrow & Co., N. Y.)

SHANGRI-LA RIFFLE

CERTAINLY, we knew now that the steady rain would bring up the big fish from below into our Shangri-La Riffle, on the Klamath (Calif.). I could imagine dozens of them working up through the swift current before me. They would probably swim deep as big steelhead do, and I longed for some magical means, as steelhead anglers always wish, to get my big fly deeper. Seldom can it get down more than a few inches in swift water, but we think that fish lying below may often see the flash and follow it around in its wide arc before taking—or rejecting—the fly.

So I cast an upstream loop, feeding out slack line, and saw my fly sucked down deeper in the wide, powerful swirls. Already the river was clouding from the heavy rain up the canyon, and I wondered if a fish could see even my big, white-winged Carson fly. Then almost on a slack line, as the fly churned opposite me, I felt a slow strong pull, much as if it had been stopped by a floating log. But this was a steelhead and a big one! It at once tore off downstream toward Hal Sackett, taking nearly one hundred yards of line before I dared try to wade out of the treacherous water.

Luckily it stopped a moment to chug and buck far below, and I dutifully and gladly ran down the bar cranking in as much line as I could. Rain clouded my glasses, and the rocks were greasy with wet slime. But the Red gods smiled, and I steadily gained on that fish without once falling down. I passed Hal, who whooped mightily, then found my fish turning back upriver, after a mighty rolling and threshing on the surface. A great leap on a bag of slack line almost stopped my racing heart, but the hook held and I had the advantage, with the steelhead fighting the current as well as my powerful rod. It came back once, then dogged down deep and held to the bottom until my sharp hammering on the rod butt goaded it into renewed fighting.

Later—a half hour after the start of the battle, Hal told me—I had this game warrior coming in to the bar. I retreated back on the rocks, rod held high and ready for that occasional last desperate dash, but this savage battler was through. Motionless, it lay on its side while I slowly slid it over the wet cobblestones.

Claude M. Kreider: STEELHEAD, 1948.
(G. P. Putnam's Sons, New York)

DUNCAN GRANT'S SALMON:

IN THE month of July, some thirty years ago, one Duncan Grant, a shoemaker by profession, who was more addicted to fishing than to his craft, went up the way from the village of Aberlour, in the north, to take a cast in some of the pools above Elchieswater. He had no great choice of tackle, as may be conceived; nothing, in fact, but what was useful, and scant supply of that.

Duncan tried one or two pools without success, till he arrived at a very deep and rapid stream, facetiously termed "the Montebank"; here he paused, as if meditating whether he should throw his line or not.

"She is very big," said he to himself, "but I'll try her; if I grip him he'll be worth the hauding."

He then fished it, a step and a throw, about half way down, when a heavy splash proclaimed that he had raised him, though he missed the fly. Going back a few paces, he came over him again, and hooked him. The first tug verified to Duncan his prognostication, that if he was there "he would be worth the hauding;" but his tackle had thirty plies of hair next the fly, and he held fast, nothing daunted.

Give and take went on with dubious advantage, the fish occasionally sulking. The thing at length became serious; and, after a succession of the same tactics, Duncan found himself at the Boat of Aberlour, seven hours after he had hooked his fish, the said fish fast under a stone, and himself completely tired. He had some thoughts of breaking his tackle and giving the thing up, but he finally hit upon an expedient to rest himself, and at the same time to guard against the surprise and consequence of a sudden movement of the fish.

He laid himself down comfortably on the banks, the butt end of his rod in front, and most ingeniously drew out part of his line, which he held in his teeth.

"If he rugs when I'm sleeping," said he, "I think I'll find him noo;" and no doubt it is probable that he would.

Accordingly, after a comfortable nap of three or four hours, Duncan was awoke by a most unceremonious tug at his jaws. In a moment he was on his feet, his rod well up, and the fish swattering down the stream. He followed as best he could, and was beginning to think of the rock at Craigellachie, when he found to his great relief that he could "get a pull on him." He had now comparatively easy work; and exactly twelve hours after hooking him, he cleiked him at the head of Lord Fife's water; he weighed fifty-four pounds, Dutch, and had the tide lice upon him.

William Scrope: DAYS AND NIGHTS OF SALMON-FISHING, 1843.
(James Blackwood & Co., Ltd.)

STEELHEAD STRIKE

ONE September, Reuben Helm and I were putting in the whole day down in the canyon of Wind River, Washington, above the suspension bridge. Shortly before noon we had climbed up on to the steep cliff at the Rock pool to look over the steelhead. The day had been a mixture of overcast and sunshine and the fish had been very active. Three of them, as we watched, moved away from their group and settled down close to our side of the river in the upper riffle.

"I'm going to try for them," I told Rube, "if you don't mind giving me directions from up here."

He consented, so I slid down the steep rock, climbed around its jutting point, and hugging the bank closely I carefully worked my way up to where the fish were resting in a small pocket. There was a large rock that I could kneel behind which would hide the movement of my rod. I stripped line into the basket and made a short cast out into the stream.

"They're still there," yelled Rube, who could see everything below the the surface with the aid of Polaroid glasses. The water was gin clear, and the fish were wary and very nervous.

"Drop your fly about twenty-five feet straight out and let it drift down," directed Rube.

I did so but nothing happened.

"Your fly stays too near the surface and doesn't sink until it gets way past the fish," called out my partner, "cast further out and more upstream."

I tried this, still kneeling behind the rock where I was in such a position that I could see neither my drifting fly or the steelhead themselves.

"Your fly's coming right over them now," yelled Rube, "one of 'em is coming right at it. Yes—no—he turned away just before he touched the fly and all of the fish have headed out into the current."

Reuben had me so worked-up over the possibilities of one of the lunkers sucking in my fly that I dropped my next back cast and hung up a bush behind me. The next several minutes were spent in loosening the line and getting the tangle out of my basket.

"I'm going to cast way out in the current and let my fly drift," I called out. The fly whipped out toward the other bank and started working downstream.

"I can see your fly," hollered Rube (it was a polar shrimp), "but no fish anywhere. But hey—wait—I can see a fish—about 30 feet upstream. It's coming—a big one—right on the dead run. Whee-e! It took your fly on the run without stopping and is heading downstream like a bullet. Watch yourself!"

That I did.

The smashing strike almost tore the rod out of my hand and the surplus line started whipping out of the basket and then off the screaming reel. The mad dash continued until the line was into the backing, when it slackened off as the steelhead leaped out of the water. All this happened in a few seconds. If I had neglected to straighten out the line before the cast the fish would have broken off at once. But it was securely hooked and came to the beach after a fast and furious fight.

Enos Bradner: NORTHWEST ANGLING, 1950.
(A. S. Barnes & Co., Inc., N. Y.)

THROW YOUR ROD IN

IF HE prove a large fish, pull not, but hold your Rod still, the butt end outward towards the fish, till you can turn him as one would turn an unruly horse. But if he will run out a stretch, and you cannot follow him, then if the place be clear, throw your Rod in after him, and commend all to Fortune, rather than lose hook, line and fish.

Robert Howlett: THE ANGLER'S SURE GUIDE, 1706.

DIFFICULTIES

THE MOST exciting encounter with a large, strong fish, I ever engaged in, took place on Teviot. The reel ordinarily used by me happened to be out of order, and I had substituted for it, without taking the precaution of examining the state of the handle, one which had been laid aside for an indefinite period. After setting up my rod and attaching the casting line and fly, I commenced operations at the head of a well-known salmon-cast, the Nine-wells, along the edge of which the wading, where it can be accomplished, is deep and unequal.

I had not taken above three or four throws, when the nut or screw by which the handle of the reel was fastened on, becoming detached, the handle itself, by the force of my throw across the pool, was precipitated forwards and lodged among some large stones lying at a depth of nearly five feet, and at a corresponding distance from the spot which I occupied when making the cast. It was some time before I could detect where it lay, and nearly an hour passed before I succeeded, by means of a large hook fastened to a stick, in recovering it. Although I had regained possession of the handle, I was unable, from want of the nut, to make active use of it in the way of recovering line. I could still manage, however, to apply it in the manner of a watch-key, so as to accomplish a few revolutions at a time, when it would invariably become detached and require replacement.

Under this drawback I recommenced fishing, using as a fly the silver-doctor. Before long, the gleam of a large salmon in the act of seizing my hook discovered itself below the surface. Raising my rod, I felt that I had him fast, not by the mouth, however, but, as it turned out, by the tough skin which lies under the pectoral fin on one side.

After the pause of a second or two, off he set at a tremendous pace up the pool, exhausting, at the first rush, nearly my whole supply of line, about seventy yards, and concluding the heat with a vigorous somersault. He then, after another short pause doubled in upon me in such a way as completely to slacken the reins, and compel me, in order to retain the master-hand, to use speed in an opposite direction; nor was it until a minute or two of high excitement had passed, that I became satisfied as to the fact that we were still in firm conjunction.

The only resource left me was to make use, as I was best able, of the loose reel-handle, and recover line as quickly as possible. This, to a certain extent, I had succeeded in doing, when the fish again set off at steam-speed on a cruise down the river. To humor this movement, I was compelled not only to follow as fast as the nature of the bank permitted, but to pay out the larger portion of my recovered line, in doing which the handle of the reel was again thrown off and fell, lost to view among the rank grass. Taken up, as I was, with my fish and his vagaries, I had no time to search for it, but marking the whereabouts of its fall, hurried, or rather was dragged, forwards in rear of the chase, the respectful distance of seventy yards being kept up betwixt us.

Still the salmon pressed on, but at a more leisurely rate, and, to keep pace with him in his way towards the foot of the pool, I had to pass my rod across the stems of several trees and bushes; also to hold it low, and in a direction nearly parallel to the water in order to avoid coming into contact with the branch-work overhead. On reaching the shallows which divide the Nine-wells from the Turnpool stream, the fish once more doubled rapidly in upon me, skimming the surface, as he did so, and making the water fly on all sides of him.

To keep a *taut* line, I had again, with all possible speed, to retrace my steps upwards, and managed at length, in spite of a good deal of maneuvering on his part, to arrive at the place where my reel-handle had been jerked off. Fortunately, I stumbled on the object of my search, and notwithstanding that I could only derive slow and imperfect assistance from it in the way of winding-up, it was to its recovery alone that I owed, after a protracted and exhausting contest, my good fortune in securing what turned out to be a fine newly-run male salmon of twenty pounds' weight. The casting-line, I may mention, was of single gut, and the hook of size No. 8 in Philips' arrangement.

Thomas Tod Stoddart: AN ANGLER'S RAMBLES, 1866.
(James Blackwood & Co., Ltd.)

The Tranquility

FYSSHYNGE WYTH AN ANGLE

THUS me semyth that huntynge and hawkynge and also fowlynge ben
so laborous and greuous that none of theym maye perfourme nor bi very
meane that enduce a man to a mery spyryte: whyche is cause of his longe
lyfe accordynge unto ye sayd parable of Salamon: Dowteles thenne folowyth
it that it must nedes be the dysporte of fysshynge wyth an angle.

For all other manere of fysshynge is also laborous and greuous; often
makynge folkes full wete and colde, whyche many tymes hath he seen
cause of grete Infirmytees. But the angler maye haue no colde nor no
dysease nor angre, but yf he be causer hymself. For he maye not lese at
the moost but a lyne or an hoke; of whyche he may hauue store plentee of
his owne makynge, as this symple treatyse shall teche hym.

So thenne his losse is not greuous, and other greyffes may he not haue,
sauynge but yf ony fisshe breke away after that he is take on the hoke, or
elles that he catche nought; whyche ben not greuous. For yf he faylle of
one he maybe not fayle of a nother, yf he dooth as this treatyse techyth;
but yf there be nought in the water.

43

And yet atte the leest he hath his holsom walke and mery at his ease, a swete ayre of the swete fauoure of the meede floures; that makyth hym hungry. He hereth the melodyous armony of fowles. He seeth the yonge swannes, heerons, duckes, cotes, and many other foules wyth theyr brodes; whyche me semyth better than alle the noyse of houndys; the blastes of hornys and the scrye of foulis that hunters; fawkeners and foulers can make.

And yf the angler take fysshe; surely thenne is there noo man merier than he is in his spyryte.

Also who soo woll use the game of anglynge; he must ryse erly, whyche thyng is prouffytable to man in this wyse, That is to wyte; moost to the heele of his Soule. For it shall cause him to be holy, and to the heele of his body. For it shall cause him to be hole. Also to the encrease of his goodys. For it shall make hym ryche. As the olde englysshe prouerbe sayth in this wyse, who soo woll ryse erly shall be holy helthy and zely. Thus have I prouyd in myn entent that the dysporte and game of anglynge is the very meane and cause that enducith a man in to a mery spyryte.

THE BOKE OF ST. ALBANS, 1496.

WHEN FISHING IS TOO GOOD

I SUPPOSE it is heresy, but I believe that fish may sometimes spoil the fishing. I remember a crisp November day on a mountain lake in the Rockies. Ice needles had grown into a jagged platform around the shore. We launched a rowboat with difficulty and trolled all day with water freezing on the line.

Fishing was never better. Large trout and silver salmon struck the bait before all the line was out. We were too busy to feel the cold and too busy to enjoy the fishing. For after all is said for the fish, there must be some time left for contemplation if the fishing is to be successful. We had no time to watch the muskrats playing on the icy shore. The flame of the quacking aspens, the flight of wild ducks, the changing beauty of sky and water did not exist for us. Even the fish lay crushed and unnoticed beneath our feet. We saw and thought nothing but the gory business of capture. We caught the fish but lost the fishing.

Far different was the effect of another day spent on the same lake. It was a summer evening and I was staying at the lodge of a land-locked captain of a Carolina turpentine boat. Tuberculosis had driven the old fellow from the sea to this remote mountain fastness. Fishermen had gathered and talk hummed about the campfire. Each angler defended his favorite lure and boasted of the fish he should catch on the morrow. The captain contributed a few guarded observations. He was dedicated to the happiness of his guests.

After the others had retired, I asked the captain in confidence just how the fish were biting.

"Well," he answered, "right now they are a bit fussy. They may take a 'Bass-Oreno,' and they may take 'Cow-bells,' and they may take a 'Daredevlet,' but they probably won't take anything."

He was right. The day was warm and still, and so were the fish. Now, one of the most solemn delusions of fishermen is that nature can be coerced. Yet sweet reasonableness comes at times to us all. The sun was so warm and friendly, the air so good, the world so still. Perhaps I can be forgiven for winding up my tackle and pulling the boat into a reed bed. I stayed there for hours while little waves made soft music on the shore. I know no better way than this of finding the peace that all men seek. I watched a king-fisher snapping up minnows off the shoals, and admired the perfection of his technique. But I did not envy him, for hunger had driven the fun from his fishing. That evening I returned to the lodge fishless but satisfied with my catch.

John Hodgdon Bradley: FAREWELL THOU BUSY WORLD, 1935.
(Primavera Press).

POSSESSED IN QUIETNESS

No LIFE, my honest scholar, no life so happy and so pleasant as the life of a well-governed angler; for when the lawyer is swallowed up with business, and the statesman is preventing or contriving plots, then we sit on cowslip-banks, hear the birds sing, and possess ourselves in as much quietness as these silent silver streams, which we now see glide so quietly by us.

Izaak Walton: THE COMPLEAT ANGLER, 1653.

THE BEST LIFE OF ANY

O the gallant fisher's life,
 It is the best of any!
'Tis full of pleasure, void of strife,
 And 'tis beloved by many:
   Other joys
   Are but toys;
   Only this
   Lawful is;
   For our skill
   Breeds no ill,
 But content and pleasure.

In the morning up we rise
 Ere Aurora's peeping;
Drink a cup to wash our eyes;
 Leave the luggard sleeping.
   Then we go
   To an fro
   With our knacks
   At our backs
   To such streams
   As the Thames,
 If we have the leisure.

When we please to walk abroad
 For our recreation,
In the fields is our abode,
 Full of delectation:
   Where in a brook,
   With a hook,
   Or a lake,
   Fish we take;
   There we sit
   For a bit,
 Till we fish entangle.

THE TRANQUILITY

We have gentles in a horn,
We have paste and worms too;
We can watch both night and morn,
Suffer rain and storms too,
None do here,
Use to swear;
Oaths do fray
Fish away;
We sit still
And watch our quill;
Fishers must not wrangle.

If the sun's excessive heat
Make our bodies swelter,
To an osier-hedge we get
For a friendly shelter;
Where in a dike,
Perch or pike,
Roach or dace,
We do chase;
Bleak or gudgeon,
Without grudging:
We are still contented.

Or we sometimes pass an hour
Under a green willow,
That defends us from a shower—
Making earth our pillow:
Where we may
Think and pray,
Before death
Stops our breath:
Other joys
Are but toys,
And to be lamented.

John Chalkhill (Perhaps Izaak Walton). Printed in THE COMPLEAT ANGLER, 1653.

THIS HUNGRY, ANGRY AGE

Old Izaak, in this angry age of ours—
This hungry, angry age—how oft of thee
We dream, and thy divine tranquility;
And all thy pleasure in the dewy flowers,
The meads enamelled and the singing showers,
And shelter of the silvery willow-tree,
By quiet waters of the river Lea!
Ah, happy hours! we cry—ah, Halcyon hours!
Yet thou, like us, hadst trouble for this realm
Of England: for thy dear Church mocked and rent,
Thy friends in beggary, thy monarch slain,
But naught could thy mild spirit overwhelm.
Ah Father Izaak, teach us thy content
When time brings many a sorrow back again.

Andrew Lang, 1844-1912. TO IZAAK WALTON.
(Longmans Green & Co., Ltd.)

PATIENCE OF JOB

"WHAT A delightful thing is fishing!" have I more than once heard some knowing angler exclaim, who, with "the patience of Job," stands or slowly moves along some rivulet twenty feet wide, and three or four feet deep, with a sham fly to allure a trout, which, when at length caught, weighs half a pound.

Reader, I never had such patience. Although I have waited ten years, and yet see only three-fourths of the Birds of America engraved, although some of the drawings of that work were patiently made so long ago as 1805, and although I have to wait with patience two years more before I see the end of it, I never could hold a line or a rod for many minutes, unless I had—not a "nibble," but a hearty bite, and could throw the fish at once over my head on the ground.

No, no—if I fish for trout, I must soon give up, or catch, as I have done in Pennsylvania's Lehigh, or the streams of Maine, fifty or more in a couple of hours.

John J. Audubon: ORNITHOLOGICAL BIOGRAPHY, 1835.

COUNTRY CONTENTMENTS

PISCATOR: . . . But turn out of the way a little, good scholar, toward yonder high honeysuckle hedge; there we'll sit and sing, whilst this shower falls so gently upon the teeming earth, and gives yet a sweeter smell to the lovely flowers that adorn these verdant meadows.

Look! under that broad beech-tree I sat down, when I was last this way a-fishing; and the birds in the adjoining grove seemed to have a friendly contention with an echo, whose dead voice seemed to live in a hollow tree, near to the brow of that primrose hill; there I sat viewing the silver streams glide silently towards their centre, the tempestuous sea; yet sometimes opposed by rugged roots, and pebble-stones, which broke their waves, and turned them into foam: and sometimes I beguiled time by viewing the harmless lambs, some leaping securely in the cool shade, whilst others sported themselves in the cheerful Sun; and saw others craving comfort from the swollen udders of their bleating dams. As I thus sat, these and other sights had so fully possessed my soul with content, that I thought, as the poet has happily expressed it,

> "I was for that time lifted above earth,
> And possessed joys not promised in my birth."

As I left this place and entered into the next field, a second pleasure entertained me; 't was a handsome Milkmaid that had not yet attained so much age and wisdom as to load her mind with any fears of many things that will never be, as too many men too often do; but she cast away all care, and sung like a nightingale. Her voice was good, and the ditty fitted for it; 't was that smooth song, which was made by Kit Marlowe, now at least fifty years ago: and the Milkmaid's mother sung an answer to it, which was made by Sir Walter Raleigh in his younger days.

They were old-fashioned poetry, but choicely good, I think much better than the strong lines that are now in fashion in this critical age. Look yonder! on my word, yonder they both be a-milking again. I will give her the Chub, and persuade them to sing those two songs to us.

God speed you, good woman! I have been a-fishing, and am going to Bleak Hall to my bed; and having caught more fish than will sup myself and my friend, I will bestow this upon you and your daughter, for I use to sell none.

MILKWOMAN: Marry, God requite you! Sir, and we'll eat it cheerfully;

and if you come this way a-fishing two months hence, a grace of God, I'll give you a syllabub of new verjuice in a new-made hay-cock for it, and my Maudlin shall sing you one of her best ballads; for she and I both love all Anglers, they be such honest, civil, quiet men. In the meantime will you drink a draught of red cow's milk? You shall have it freely.

PISCATOR: No, I thank you; but I pray do us a courtesy that shall stand you and your daughter nothing, and yet we will think ourselves still something in your debt: it is but to sing us a song that was sung by your daughter when I last passed over this meadow, about eight or nine days since.

MILKWOMAN: What song was it, I pray? Was it "Come, Shepherds, deck your herds"? or, "As at noon Dulcina rested"? or "Phillida flouts me"? or "Chevy Chace?" or "Johnny Armstrong?" or "Troy Town?"

PISCATOR: No, it is none of these: it is a song that your daughter sung the first part, and you sung the answer to it.

MILKWOMAN: O, I know it now; I learned the first part in my golden age, when I was about the age of my poor daughter; and the latter part, which indeed fits me best now, but two or three years ago, when the cares of the world began to take hold of me: but you shall, God willing, hear them both, and sung as well as we can, for we both love Anglers. Come, Maudlin, sing the first part to the gentlemen with a merry heart, and I'll sing the second, when you have done:

The Milkmaid's Song

"Come, live with me, and be my love,
And we will all the pleasures prove
That valleys, groves, or hills, or fields
Or woods and steepy mountains yields.

"Where we will sit upon the rocks,
And see the shepherds feed our flocks,
By shallow rivers, to whose falls
Melodious birds sing madrigals.

"And I will make thee beds of roses,
And then a thousand fragrant posies;
A cap of flowers, and a kirtle
Embroidered all with leaves of myrtle,

"A gown made of the finest wool,
Which from our pretty lambs we pull;
Slippers lined choicely for the cold,
With buckles of the purest gold;

"A belt of straw, and ivy-buds,
With coral clasps and amber studs;—
And if these pleasures may thee move,
Come, live with me, and be my love.

"Thy silver dishes for thy meat,
As precious as the Gods do eat,
Shall on an ivory table be
Prepared each day for thee and me.

"The shepherd swains shall dance and sing
For thy delight each May morning:
If these delights thy mind may move,
Then live with me, and be my love."

VENATOR: Trust me, Master, it is a choice song, and sweetly sung by honest Maudlin. I now see it was not without cause that our good Queen Elizabeth did so often wish herself a Milkmaid all the month of May, because they are not troubled with fears and cares, but sing sweetly all the day and sleep securely all the night: and, without doubt, honest, innocent, pretty Maudlin does so. I'll bestow Sir Thomas Overbury's milkmaid's wish upon her,—"that she may die in the Spring; and, being dead, may have good store of flowers stuck round about her winding-sheet."

THE MILKMAID'S MOTHER'S ANSWER

"If all the world and love were young,
And truth in every shepherd's tongue,
These pretty pleasures might me move
To live with thee, and be thy love.

"But Time drives flocks from field to fold:
When rivers rage, and rocks grow cold,
Then Philomel becometh dumb,
And age complains of cares to come.

51

"The flowers do fade, and wanton fields
To wayward Winter reckoning yields:
A honey tongue, a heart of gall,
Is fancy's spring, but sorrow's fall.

"Thy gowns, thy shoes, thy beds of roses,
Thy cap, thy kirtle, and thy posies,
Soon break, soon wither, soon forgotten;
In folly ripe, in reason rotten.

"Thy belt of straw, and ivy-buds,
Thy coral clasps and amber studs,
All these in me no means can move
To come to thee, and be thy Love.

"What should we talk of dainties then,
Of better meat than's fit for men?
These are but vain: that's only good
Which God hath blest, and sent for food.

"But could youth last, and love still breed,
Had joys no date, nor age no need,—
Then those delights my mind might move,
To live with thee, and be thy love."

MOTHER: Well, I have done my song. But stay, honest Anglers, for I will make Maudlin sing you one short song more. Maudlin, sing that song that you sung last night, when young Coridon the Shepherd played so purely on his oaten pipe to you and your Cousin Betty.

MAUDLIN: I will, Mother.

"I married a wife of late,
The more's my unhappy fate:
I married her for love,
As my fancy did me move,
And not for a worldly estate:

"But oh! the green-sickness
Soon changed her likeness,
And all her beauty did fail.
But 't is not so
With those that go
Through frost and snow,
As all men know,
And carry the milking-pail."

PISCATOR: Well sung! Good woman, I thank you. I'll give you another dish of fish one of these days; and then beg another song of you. Come, Scholar, let Maudlin alone: do not you offer to spoil her voice. Look! yonder comes mine Hostess, to call us to supper. How now! is my brother Peter come?

HOSTESS: Yes, and a friend with him; they are both glad to hear that you are in these parts, and long to see you, and long to be at supper, for they be very hungry.

Izaak Walton: THE COMPLEAT ANGLER, 1653.

HARD-BOILED EGGS AND AMBER ALE

NEAR the ford is the choicest spot for luncheon that Nature ever devised. Five big trees, chestnut, elm, ash, oak, and beech, there combine to ward off the sun, and then the stream, always in the shade, babbles round three corners with the impetousness of a mountain brook. With a brace in the creel, or without it, an angler could never fail in that spot of a divine content. Hard-boiled eggs, a crisp lettuce, bread and butter, and a bottle of amber ale a-cool in the water at his feet—what could appetite want better in so smiling a corner of the world?

Hugh T. Sheringham, TROUT FISHING, 1920.
(Hodder & Stoughton)

Pleasures Attending

I COULD SIT QUIETLY

THAT very hour which you were absent from me, I sat down under a willow-tree by the water-side, and considered what you had told me of the owner of that pleasant meadow in which you then left me; that he had a plentiful estate, and not a heart to think so; that he had at this time many lawsuits depending; and that they both damped his mirth, and took up so much of his time and thoughts, that he himself had not leisure to take the sweet content that I, who pretended no title to them, took in his fields: for I could sit quietly; and looking on the water, see some fishes sport themselves in the silver streams, others leaping at flies of several shapes and colors; looking on the hills, I could behold them spotted with woods and groves; looking down the meadows, could see, here a boy gathering lilies and lady-smocks, and there a girl cropping culverkeys and cowslips, all to make garlands suitable to this present month of May.

Izaak Walton: THE COMPLEAT ANGLER, 1653.

GREEN GRASS

In this lone, open glade I lie,
Screen'd by deep boughs on either hand;
And at its end, to stay the eye,
Those black-crown'd, red-boled pine trees stand!

Birds here make song, each bird has his,
Across the girdling city's hum;
How green under the boughs it is!
How thick the tremulous sheep-cries come!

Here at my feet what wonders pass,
What endless, active life is here!
What blowing daisies, fragrant grass!
An air-stirr'd forest, fresh and clear.

Scarce fresher is the mountain-sod
Where the tired angler lies, stretch'd out,
And, eased of basket and of rod,
Counts his day's spoil, the spotted trout.

Matthew Arnold: LINES WRITTEN IN KENSINGTON GARDENS, 1852.
(The Macmillan Co., N. Y.)

ALL'S RIGHT

The year's at the spring
And day's at the morn;
Morning's at seven;
The hill-side's dew-pearled;
The lark's on the wing;
The snail's on the thorn;
God's in his heaven—
All's right with the world!

Robert Browning: PIPPA PASSES, 1841.
(John Murray, Ltd.)

THE FOREST FAIR

On Ettrick Forest's mountains dun
'Tis blithe to hear the sportsman's gun,
And seek the heath-frequenting brood
Far through the noonday solitude;
By many a cairn and trenched mound
Where chiefs of yore sleep lone and sound,
And springs where grey-haired shepherds tell
That still the fairies love to dwell.

Along the silver streams of Tweed
'Tis blithe the mimic fly to lead,
When to the hook the salmon springs
And the line whistles through the rings;
The boiling eddy see him try,
Then dashing from the current high,
Till watchful eye and cautious hand
Have led his wasted strength to land.

'Tis blithe along the midnight tide
With stalwart arm the boat to guide,
On high the dazzling blaze to rear,
And heedful plunge the barbed spear;
Rock, wood, and scaur emerging bright
Fling on the stream their ruddy light,
And from the bank our band appears
Like Genii, arm'd with fiery spears.

'Tis blithe at eve to tell the tale,
How we succeed, and how we fail,
Whether at Alwyn's lordly meal,
Or lowlier board of Ashiestiel;
While the gay tapers cheerly shine,
Bickers the fire, and flows the wine—
Days free from thought, and nights from care,
My blessing on the Forest fair!

Sir Walter Scott: LIFE IN THE FOREST, 1822.

THE CALM, QUIET, INNOCENT RECREATION OF ANGLING

WE MAY say of angling as Dr. Boteler said of strawberries: "Doubtless God could have made a better berry, but doubtless God never did," and so, if I might be judge, God never did make a more calm, quiet innocent recreation than angling.

Izaak Walton: THE COMPLEAT ANGLER, 1653.

BEHOLD, THE PRIZE IS THINE

When floating clouds their spongy fleeces drain,
Troubling the streams with swift-descending rain.
And waters, tumbling down the mountain's side,
Bear the loose soil into the swelling tide;
Then, soon as vernal gales begin to rise,
And drive the liquid burthen thro' the skies,
The fisher to the neighboring current speeds,
Whose rapid surface purls, unknown to weeds;
Upon a rising border of the brook
He sits him down, and ties the treach'rous hook;
Now expectation cheers his eager thought,
His bosom glows with treasures yet uncaught,
Before his eyes a banquet seems to stand,
Where ev'ry guest applauds his skillful hand.

Far up the stream the twisted hair he throws,
Which down the murm'ring current gently flows;
When if or chance or hunger's powerful sway
Directs the roving trout this fatal way,
He greedily sucks in the twining bait,
And tugs and nibbles the fallacious meat:
Now, happy fisherman, now twitch the line!
How thy rod bends! behold, the prize is thine!

John Gay, RURAL SPORTS, 1713.

PLEASANT'ST ANGLING

The pleasant'st angling is to see the fish
Cut with her golden oars the silver stream,
And greedily devour the treacherous bait.

William Shakespeare: MUCH ADO ABOUT NOTHING, 1598.

ANGLING CARRIETH NEITHER COVETOUSNESSE, DECEIPT, NOR ANGER

SINCE Pleasure is a Rapture, or power in this last Age, stolne into the hearts of men, and there lodged up with such a carefull guard and attendance, that nothing is more Supreme, or ruleth with greater strength in their affections, and since all are now become the sonnes of Pleasure, and every good is measured by the delight it produceth: what worke unto men can be more thankful then the Discourse of that pleasure which is most comely, most honest, and giveth the most liberty to Divine Meditation? And that without all question is the Art of Angling, which having ever bin most hurtlesly necessary, hath bin the sport or Recreation of Gods Saints, of most holy Fathers, and of many worthy and Reverend Divines, both dead, and at this time breathing.

For the use thereof (in its owne true and unabused nature) carrieth in it neither covetousnesse, deceipt, nor anger, the three maine spirits which (ever in some ill measure) rule in all other pastimes, neither are alone predominant without the attendance of their severall handmaides, as Theft, Blasphemy or Bloodshed: for in Dice-play, Cards, Bowles, or any other sport where money is the goale to which mens minds are directed, what can mans avarice there be accounted, other than a familiar Robbery, each seeking by deceit to couzen and spoile other of that blisse of menes which God had bestowed to support them and their families? And as in every contention there must be a betterhook or super-excelling, so in this, when the weaker deceit is deprived his expectation, how doth it then fall into curses, oathes, and furies, such as would make Vertue tremble with the imagination.

But in this Art of Angling there is no such evill, no such sinfull violence, for the greatest thing it coveteth, is for much labour a little Fish, hardly so much as will suffice Nature in a reasonale stomack: for the Angler must intice, not command his reward, and that which is worthy millions to his contentment, another may buy for a groate in the market. His deceipt worketh not upon men but upon those creatures whom it is lawful to beguile for our honest recreations or needful uses, and for all rage and fury it must be so great a stranger to this civill pastime, that if it come but within view of speculation thereof, it no more to be esteemed a Pleasure, for every proper good thereof in the very instant faileth, shewing until all men that will undergoe any delight therein, that it was first invented, taught, and shall for ever been maintained by Patience onely.

And yet I may not say onely Patience, for her other three Sisters have likewise a commanding power in this exercise, for Justice directeth and appointeth out those places where men may with liberty use their sport, and neither do injury to their neighbors, nor incure the censure of incivillity. Temperance layeth downe the measure of the action, and moderateth desire in such good proportion, that no Excesse is found in the overflow of their affections. Lastly, Fortitude inableth the minde to undergo the travaile, and exchange of Weathers with a healthfull ease, and not to dispaire with a little expence of time, but to persevere with a constant imagination in the end to obtain both pleasure and satisfaction.

Gervase Markham (1568-1637): COUNTRY CONTENTMENTS

THEN TO ANGLE WE WILL GO

Of all the Sports and Pastimes
Which happen in the Year,
To Angling there are none, sure,
That ever can compare;

We do not break our Legs or Arms
As Huntsmen often do;
For when that we are Angling
No Danger can ensue.

In Westminster the Gentlemen
In Black their Conscience sell
And t'other Gentleman in Black
Will sure reward them well.

A Client is a Gudgeon
  And freely takes the Bait
A Lawyer is a Jack, and
  For him does slyly wait.

Then you who would be honest,
  And to Old Age attain,
Forsake the City and the Town
  And fill the Angler's Train.

We meddle not with State Affairs
  Or for Preferment push;
Court places and Court pensions
  We value not a Rush.

For Health and for Diversion
  We rise by Break of Day,
While Courtiers in their Down-beds
  Sweat half their Time away.

And then unto the River
  In haste we do repair;
All Day in sweet Amusement
  We breathe good wholesome Air.

Through Meadows, by a River,
  From Place to Place we roam,
And when that we are weary,
  We then go jogging Home;

At Night we take a Bottle,
  We prattle, laugh and sing;
We drink a Health unto our Friends,
  And so God bless the King.

Then to Angle we will go, will go,
  To Angle we will go.

George Smith: **THE GENTLEMAN ANGLER, 1726.**

GOOD GOD! HOW SWEET ARE ALL THINGS HERE!

Farwell, thou busy World! and may
  We never meet again:
Here can I eat, and sleep, and pray
And do more good in one short day,
Than he, who his whole age out-wears
Upon the most conspicuous theatres
  Where nought but vanity and vice appears.

Good God! how sweet are all things here!
How beautiful the fields appear!
  How cleanly do we feed and lie!
Lord! what good hours do we keep!
How quietly we sleep!
  What peace! what unanimity!
How innocent from the lewd fashion
Is all our business, all our recreation!

How calm and quiet a delight
  It is alone
To read, and meditate, and write,
  By none offended and offending none!
To walk, ride, sit, or sleep at one's own ease
And pleasing a man's self, none other to displease!

O my belov'd nymph! fair Dove;
Princess of rivers, how I love
  Upon thy flowery banks to lie
And view thy silver stream,
When gilded by a summer's beam,
  And in it all thy wanton fry
  Playing at liberty,
And with my angle upon them,
  The all of treachery
  I ever learnt, industriously to try!

Lord! would men let me alone,
What an over-happy one
* Should I think myself to be,*
Might I in this desert place,
Which most men in discourse disgrace,
* Live but undisturb'd and free!*
Here, in this despis'd recess
* Would I, maugre winter's cold,*
And the summer's worst excess,
* Try to live out to sixty full years old!*
And, all the while,
* Without an envious eye*
On any thriving under Fortune's smile
* Contented live, and then contented die.*

Charles Cotton: POEMS ON SEVERAL OCCASIONS, 1689.

Weather & When To Angle

A FAYR SONNY DAYE IS RYGHTE GOOD

FROM Septembre unto Apryll in a fayr sonny daye is ryghte good to angle. And yf the wynde in that season have ony parte of the Oryent: the wedyr thenne is nought. And whan it is a grete wynde, and when it snowith reynyth or hayllyth, or is a grete tempeste, as thondyr or lightenynge: or a hote weder: thenne it is noughte for to angle.

THE BOKE OF ST. ALBANS, 1496

SABBATH FISHING?

HAS it ever struck you that the trouts bite best on the Sabbath? God's critters tempting decent men.

James Matthew Barrie, 1860-1937: THE LITTLE MINISTER.
(Charles Scribner's Sons, N. Y.)

THE ANGLER'S INVITATION

Come when the leaf comes, angle with me,
Come when the bee hums over the lea,
  Come with the wild flowers,
  Come with the mild showers,
Come when the singing bird calleth for thee!

Then to the stream side, gladly we'll hie,
Where the grey trout glide silently by,
  Or in some still place
  Over the hill face
Hurrying onward, drop the light fly.

Then, when the dew falls, homeward we'll speed
To our own loved walls down on the mead,
  There, by the bright hearth,
  Holding our night mirth,
We'll drink to sweet friendship in need and in deed.

Thomas Tod Stoddard: ANGLING SONGS, 1889.
(James Blackwood & Co., Ltd.)

A GREAT STORM COMING UP

ONE burn I used to fish which flowed through a wood of high trees down a steep rocky channel. Here it was possible, at least for a small boy, to keep out of sight by walking up the bed of the burn itself, stooping low, jerking the worm up into little pools and cascades above, and lifting the trout out down stream on to the bank. This was very pretty work.

I remember once getting several trout quickly one after the other in this place, and then they suddenly stopped taking. One little favourite pool after another produced nothing, and a fear of something unknown came over me; the gloom and stillness of the wood made me uneasy, everything about me seemed to know something, to have a meaning which was hidden from me; and I felt as if my fishing was out of place.

At last I could resist the feeling of apprehension no longer; I left the rod with the line in a pool to fish for itself, and went up to the edge of the wood to see what was happening in the open world outside. There was a great storm coming up full of menace, as thunderclouds often are. It filled me with terror. I hurried back for my rod, left the burn and the wood, and fled before the storm, going slow to get breath now and then, and continually urged to running again by the sound of thunder behind me.

Lord Grey of Fallodon: FLY FISHING, 1899.
(A. P. Watt and Son)

SIGNS OF RAIN

If Ducks at their first rising and standing on their feet, do flutter and flap their wings.

If swallows flutter, and fly low over land or water, and beat the water with their wings.

If sparrows chirp much in a fair morning.

If cattle bellow, puff, and look up to the sky.

If sheep bleat, or skip and play wontonly.

If swine carry hay, straw, etc., to hide it.

If dog's guts rumble.

If moles cast up earth more than ordinary, and the earth they cast be small and dry.

If frogs croak more than commonly they do.

If toads make from their holes in the evening.

If worms come quite out of the earth, more than they use to do.

If pismires or ants run often to their nests.

If flies or fleas bite or sting worse than they wont.

If flies hover about the mouths and eyes of people or beasts.

If solid bodies, as stone, wainscoat, etc. do sweat or make a crackling noise.

If powder'd meat becomes more moist than's usual.

If soot falls down the chimney more than ordinary, not being very foul.

If the sounds of bells be heard farther and plainer than at other times, without the help of the wind.

If aches, hurts of corns do pain or grieve more than they wont to do.

Robert Howlett: THE ANGLER'S SURE GUIDE, 1706.

CATCH FISH, IF YOU CAN

WHEN Mr. *Brock* lived in the *Isle of Sholes,* he brought the People into an Agreement, that, besides the *Lord's-Day* they would spend one Day every Month together in the Worship of our Lord Jesus Christ. On a certain Day, which by their Agreement belong'd unto the Exercies of Religion, being arrived, the Fishermen came to Mr. *Brock,* and ask'd him, that they might *Put by their Meeting,* and go a Fishing, because they had lost many Days, by the Foulness of the Weather.

He seeing, that without and against his Consent, they resolved upon doing what they had asked of him, replied, *If you will go away, I say unto you, catch Fish, if you can! But as for you, that will tarry, and worship the Lord Jesus Christ this Day, I will pray unto Him for you, that you may take Fish till you are weary.* Thirty Men went away from the Meeting, and *Five* tarried.

The *Thirty* which went away from the Meeting, with all their Skill could catch but *Four* fishes; the *Five* which tarried, went forth afterwards, and they took *Five* hundred. The *Fishermen* after this readily attended, whatever Meetings Mr. *Brock* appointed them.

Cotton Mather: MAGNALIA CHRISTI AMERICANA, 1702.

WHEN NOUGHT TO ANGLE

Now for those seasons which are nought to Angle in, there is none worse than in the violent heate of the day, or when the Windes are loudest, Raine heaviest, Snow and Hayle extremest; Thunder and lightning are offensive, or any sharpe ayre which flyeth from the East; the places where men use to wash Sheepe you shall for beare, for the very smell of the wool will chase fish from their haunts. Land floods are enemies to Anglers, so also at the fall of the leave is the shedding of leaves into the water, and many other such like pollutions.

Gervase Markham (1568-1637): COUNTRY CONTENTMENTS.

WASHINGTON FISHES FOR COD

HAVING lines, we proceeded to the fishing banks, a little without the harbour, and fished for Cod; but it not being a proper time of tide, we only caught two, with w'ch, about 1 o'clock, we returned to Town. Dined at Mr. Langdon's, and drank Tea there, with a large circle of Ladies, and retired a little after seven o'clock.

George Washington: WASHINGTON'S DIARY, 1789.

The Water

A RIVER'S FRIENDSHIP

WHEN one has fished a water season after season for five years, then is its friendship a great and living thing. Each feature of the long-fished stream is with one at all times—each curve and vista, each willow and withybed, the unguessable hatch-hole, the frank, revealing shallow, and the swelling downs and the distant clumps.

These things are a possession that nothing can destroy so long as memory serves.

Though paralysis should strike one into a living death, while memory were faithful one should yet wander in one's mind (by no means deliriously) through certain green water-meadows, eye busy with a certain stream where stout fish should always be rising. Its consolation would never fail.

William Caine: AN ANGLER AT LARGE, 1911.
(Routledge and Kegan Paul, Ltd.)

SWEET COQUET

Come bring to me my limber gad
 I've fish'd wi' mony a year,
An' let me hae my weel-worn creel,
 An' a' my fishing gear;
The sunbeams glint on Linden-Ha',
 The breeze comes frae the west,
An' lovely looks the gowden morn
 On the streams that I like best.

I've thrawn the flee thae sixty year,
 Ay, sixty year an' mair,
An' monie a speckled Troutie kill'd
 Wi' heckle, heuk, an' hair;
An' now I'm auld an' feeble grown,
 My locks are like the snaw,
But I'll gang again to Coquet-side,
 An' take a fareweel thraw.

O Coquet! in my youthfu' days
 Thy river sweetly ran,
An' sweetly down thy woody braes
 The bonnie birdies sang;
But streams may rin, an' birds may sing,
 Sma' joy they bring to me,
The blithesome strains I dimly hear,
 The streams I dimly see.

But, ance again, the weel-keen'd sounds
 My minutes shall beguile,
An' glistering in the airly sun
 I'll see thy waters smile;
An' Sorrow shall forget his sigh,
 An' Age forget his pain,
An' ance mair, by sweet Coquet-side,
 My heart be young again.

THE WATER

Ance mair I'll touch wi' gleesome foot
  Thy waters clear and cold,
Ance mair I'll cheat the gleg-e'ed trout,
  An' wile him frae his hold;
Ance mair, at Weldon's frien'ly door,
  I'll wind my tackle up,
An' drink "Success to Coquet-side,"
  Though a tear fa' in the cup.

An' then fareweel, dear Coquet-side!
  Aye gaily may thou rin,
An' lead thy waters sparkling on,
  An' dash frae linn to linn;
Blithe be the music o' thy streams
  An' banks through after-days,
An' blithe be every Fisher's heart
  Shall ever tread thy Braes!

Robert Roxby & Thomas Doubleday: NEWCASTLE FISHERS' GARLANDS, 1820.

A RIVER FLOWS IN EDEN

Southward through Eden went a River large,
Nor chang'd his course, but through the shaggie hill
Pass'd underneath ingulft, for God had thrown
That Mountain as his Garden mould high rais'd
Upon the rapid current, which through veins
Of porous Earth with kindly thirst up drawn,
Rose a fresh Fountain, and with many a rill
Water'd the Garden; thence united fell
Down the steep glade, and met the neather Flood,
Which from his darksom passage now appears,
And now divided into four main Streams,
Runs divers, wand'ring many a famous Realme
And Country whereof here needs no account,
But rather to tell how, if Art could tell,
How from that Saphire Fount the crisped Brooks
Rowling on Orient Pearl and sands of Gold,

With mazie error under pendant shades
Ran Nectar, visiting each plant, and fed
Flours worthy of Paradise which not nice Art
In Beds and curious Knots, but Nature boon
Powrd forth profuse on Hill and Dale and Plaine,
Both where the morning Sun first warmly smote
The open field, and where the unpierc't shade
Imbround the noontide Bowrs . . .
. . . mean while murmuring waters fall
Down the slope hills, disperst, or in a Lake,
That the fringed Bank with Myrtle crown'd,
Her chrystall mirror holds, unite their streams.

John Milton, 1608-1674, PARADISE LOST.

ADIEU TO THE RIVER

THE storm has passed away, the dripping trees are sparkling in the warm and watery sunset.

Back, then, to our inn, where dinner waits for us, the choicest of our own trout, pink as salmon, with the milky curd in them, and no sauce to spoil the delicacy of their flavour. Then bed, with its lavender-scented sheets and white curtains, and sleep, sound sweet sleep, that loves the country village and comes not near London bedroom.

In the morning adieu to Cheneys, with its red gable-ends and chimneys, its venerable trees, its old-world manners, and the solemn memories of its mausoleum.

Adieu, too, to the river, which, "though men may come and men may go," has flowed and will flow on forever, winding among its reed beds, murmuring over its gravelly fords, heedless of royal dynasties, uncaring whether Cheney or Russell calls himself lord of its waters, graciously turning the pleasant corn mills in its course, unpolluted by the fetid refuse of manufactures, and travelling on to the ocean bright and pure and uncharged with poison, as in the old times when the priest sung mass in the church upon the hill and the sweet soft matins bell woke the hamlet to its morning prayers.

James Anthony Froude, 1818-1894. CHENEYS AND THE HOUSE OF RUSSELL.
(Longmans Green & Co., Ltd.)

Methods, Precepts & Admonishments

CAST TO THE RIGHT

THERE were together Simon Peter, and Thomas called Didymus, and Nathanael of Cana in Galilee, and the sons of Zebedee, and two other of his disciples. Simon Peter saith unto them, I go afishing. They say unto him, We also go with thee. They went forth, and entered into a ship immediately; and that night they caught nothing.

But when the morning was now come, Jesus stood on the shore; but the disciples knew not that it was Jesus.

Then Jesus saith unto them, Children, have ye any meat? They answered Him, No.

And He said unto them, Cast the net on the right side of the ship, and ye shall find. They cast therefore, and now they were not able to draw it for the multitude of fishes.

THE GOSPEL ACCORDING TO ST. JOHN.

ANGLE IN SEASONABLE TIMES

YOU MUST not Angle in unseasonable times, for the Fish not being in-clined to Bite, it is a strange intisement that can compel them.

Then you must be careful neither by your apparell, motions, or too open standing to give afright to the Fish, for when they are scared they flye from you, and you seeke Society in an empty House.

Then must you labour in cleer and untroubled waters, for when the Brookes are any thing white, muddy, and thicke, either through inunda-tions or other trouble, it is impossible to get anything with the Angle: then to respect the temper of the weather, for extreme wind or extreme cold taketh from Fish all manner of appetite; So doth likewise too violent heate, or raine that is greate, heavy, and beating, or any stormes, Snowes, Hailes, or blustrings.

If you will angle for the Chub, Chevin or Trout, all your instruments must be strong and good: your rod darke and discoloured, your line strong, but small and short, your hooke of a twopenny compasse, and if you Angle with a Flye, then, nor Lead, nor Corke, nor Quill, if otherwise, then all of a handsome and suitable proportion.

The best standing to take them is in close and concealed places, as behind Trees, Walles, or Arches of Bridges: their haunts are in cleere waters which runne upon Sand or Gravell, and they are in best season from March till Michaelmas: if you Angle for them with dead Flyes, without Lead or Corke, but if you angle for them with other baites, then you must have both Corke and Lead, for he will bite neere the bottome, yet some-times you may angle for him with a small Menow hanged at your hooke by the neither parts, without Corke or Lead and so draw the bayte upon the top of the water, and both with it, and with every flye, strike rather before than after he byteth.

Gervase Markham (1568-1637): COUNTRY CONTENTMENTS.

THE TROUTE COMETH SO FAST

BUT IF ye angle for the Troute with a flye, ye shall strike when he is a foote and more from your baite, for he cometh so fast.

Leonard Mascall: A BOOKE OF FISHING WITH HOOKE AND LINE,
And Of All Other Instruments Thereunto Belonging, 1590.

THE FISH WILL TAKE YOUR BAIT WITH LESS SUSPICION

WHEN you angle in very calm, bright Weather, and in still, standing clear Water, and would not be seen of the Fish; take a dry cow-shard, and lay a quantity of Tar upon the outside of it, and set it off to lie still, just over your baited place; which, when soaked through with the Water, the Tar will diffuse, and spread all over the place, and make so thick a scum on the Water, that the Fish cannot see you but will take your Baits with less suspicion; especially if you bait the Ground near the Bak-side.

Robert Howlett, THE ANGLER'S SURE GUIDE, 1706.

USE THIS CRAFTY DYSPORTE FOR YOURE SOLACE

YE THAT can angle & take fysshe to your plesures as this forsayd treatyse techyth & Shewyth you: I charge & requyre you in the name of alle noble men that ye fysshe not in noo poore mannes seuerall (private) water: as his ponde: stewe: of other necessary thynges to kepe fysshe in, wythout his lycence & good wyll.

Also that ye breke noo mannys heggys in goynge abowte your dysportes: ne opyn noo mannes gates but that ye shytte theym agayn.

Also ye shall not use this forsayd crafty dysporte for no covetysenes to the increasynge & sparynge of youre money oonly: but pryncypally for youre solace, & to cause the helthe of your body, and specyally of youre soule, For whan ye purpose to goo on your dysportes in fysshynge, ye woll not desyre gretly many persones wyth you, whyche myghte lette you of your game. And thenne ye maye seruse (serve) God devowtly in sayenge affectuously your custumable prayer. And thus doynge ye shall eschewe & foyde many vices, as idylness, whyche is pryncypall cause to enduce man to many other vyces, as it is ryght well knowen.

Also ye shall not be rauenous in takyng of your sayd game as to moche at one tyme: whyche lyghtly be occasion to dystroye your owne dysporte & other mennes also. As when ye haue suffycyent mese ye sholde coveyte no more as at that tyme.

And all those that done after this rule shall haue the blessynge of God & Saynt Petry: whyche he theym graunte that wyth his precyous blood vs boughte.

THE BOKE OF ST. ALBANS, 1496.

WORM-FISHING UPSTREAM

CHARLES EBDY declared that worm-fishing upstream, in clear water, as a high branch of the art, was first practised by the Witton schoolboys. The earliest really successful anglers in this way of whom I ever heard were the sons of Sir William Chaytor, first Baronet of Witton Castle. These lands associating with the schoolboys, the art became common to them all, thence it spread.

Charlie himself learnt it from a Witton boy, as far back as the year 1820. It is certain that during my early visits with Charlie to Coquet Glen, Till, Tweed, and Whiteadder, commencing in 1831, we never met with or heard of anyone who fished with worm up stream, and hence our wonderful success in the months of June and July caused us to be narrowly watched by some who were desirous to learn our secret.

William Henderson: MY LIFE AS AN ANGLER, 1879.
(W. Satchell, Peyton & Co.)

RUNNING THE GADGER

THE most deadly legal method of catching trout known to me is "running the Gadger!" a method peculiar to Clyde waters; the tackle and technique probably originated within Scotland.

Select a large hand net, the mesh of which diminishes with depth. Mouth must be reinforced with a steel circle. Proceed to shallow gravel bed—stirring up the gravel with wading brogues assists—and shrimp along the bottom uplifting stones and bed in net. Inspect, picking out creepers until sufficient quantity is obtained. (In California you have a stone fly (*Pteronaryas California*) known in the Klamath river country as *The Salmon Fly*). They are quite fearsome in appearance but harmless, being available in varying sizes throughout the season excepting end of May and June when they take wing reaching imago stage.

Bind three hooks to a stout piece of gut with silk, but be careful to blend it with the creeper's coloration else no trout. No contrast will succeed. Impale the creeper on the hook with one barb through the body, a second through the thorax, leaving the third hook, opposite the thorax free as a fish-hooking aid. Attach a nine-foot leader to which a single split shot has been added nine inches from tackle. Add a *tiny* adjustable float judging depth of streams to be fished so that creeper is approximately two inches off bottom. Skill with practice enables correct depth to be ascertained. Usual 9 foot 6 inch, plus fly rod is best.

Start at head of good moving stream. Cast gently into *centre and walk or run down parallel with float*. This must be done. Immediately a fish is felt, strike smartly else you have lost your creeper.

Anyone who thinks this fishing method should be related to worm class let him have a try. Apart from energy required to keep alongside float, I have seen experienced men lose twenty odd creepers to fish, without hooking a taker. Nymphs are so fragile and trout pounce upon them:—well, just have a try! It can be marvelous sport when fly is off and does it improve your striking ability! You will be twice the dry-fly man after you can get them out with the creeper. There are always "takers" and no *dull* days.

Some competitions here are devoted entirely to "running the Gadger!" Experts average 25 to 30 fish—many secure none. For brains and hand coordination, it is wonderful training. By the way, trout prefer the large creepers which are generally female. Why I do not know, as colour of both sexes vary with surroundings. Same when flies hatch out. Sponsor a "Gadger" competition and have a laugh at the cursing when hooks are cleaned.

Thomas Clegg, 1950.

NATURE MAKES NOTHING IN VAIN

NATURE that makes nothing in vain, having given to Fish Eyes to see, Ears to hear, Nostrils to smell, and Palats to taste; the Angler should have regard to all these, viz., to keep out of sight; to make no noise; to please their scent, and humour their palats.

*　　*　　*

HE THAT angles fine, or with single Hairs, in clean, clear, and large Waters, with proper Baits, and keeps out of sight, will take five times more Fish, than he that fishes coarse, or in sight; especially, if he that fishes fine doth use a Reel on his Rod with a Running-Line, and hath a Landing-Net to land his Fish; and when he fishes for Trouts, in shallows and sharps, doth wade and fish.

Now when you angle, hold your Rod in both your Hands, one Hand just below your Tumbrel, and the thumb of that hand on the tumbrel; the other Hand above the tumbrel, and the thumb of that hand on the line and rod to keep the tumbrel from turning around, and your Line from running out when you toss out your bait, throw your flie, or strike a fish, or upon any other occasion.

Robert Howlett: THE ANGLER'S SURE GUIDE, 1607.

MASTER AND MAN

Do ye ken hoo to fush for the salmon?
  If ye'll listen I'll tell ye.
Dinna trust to the books and their gammon,
  They're but trying to sell ye.
Leave professors to read their ain cackle
  And fush their ain style;
Come awa' , sir, we'll oot wi' oor tackle
  And be busy the while.

'Tis a wee bit ower bright, ye were thinkin'?
  Aw, ye'll no be the loser;
'Tis better ten baskin' and blinkin'
  Than ane that's a cruiser.
If ye're bent, as I tak it, on slatter,
  Ye should pray for the droot,
For the salmon's her ain when there's watter,
  But she's oors when it's oot.

Ye may just put your flee-book behind ye,
  Ane hook wull be plenty;
If they'll no come for this, my man, mind ye,
  They'll no come for twenty.
Ay, a rod; but the shorter the stranger
  And the nearer to strike;
For myself I prefare it nae langer
  Than a yard or the like.

Noo, ye'll stand awa' back while I'm creepin'
Wi' my snoot i' the gowans;
There's a bonny twalve-poonder a-sleepin'
I' the shade o' yon rowans.
Man, man! I was fearin' I'd stirred her,
But I've got her the noo!
Hoot! fushin's as easy as murrder
When ye ken what to do.

Na, na, sir, I doot na ye're willin'
But I canna permit ye;
For I'm thinkin' that yon kind o' killin'
Wad hardly befit ye.
And some work is deefficult hushin',
There'd be havers and chaff:
'Twull be best, sir, for you to be fushin'
And me wi' the gaff.

Sir Henry Newbolt: POEMS: NEW AND OLD, 1912.
(A. P. Watt & Son)

Fly Fishing

THE MOST PLEASANT PART OF ANGLING

Artificial flie Angling is the most gentile, ingenious, pleasonat and profitable part of the innocent Recreation of Angling; to the perfect Accomplishment of which, is required, not only good affecttion and frequent practise, but also diligent Observation and considerable Judgment; especially in the choice of Materials and mixing of colours for flies.

Robert Howlett: THE ANGLER'S SURE GUIDE, 1706.

THE MAY FLY DANCE

There's a time of day close to the heart of every man who has floated a fly. It's the time of day when the deer leaves his bed and the rabbit his form. It's the time when all is calm, and the cool mists begin to rise; and when the crickets and katydids commence to tune their fiddles, and the bull bats zoom and roar in their power dives. In short, it's the time when the May flies dance.

This is a time of action; for when a heavy hatch is on, all the fish in the stream gorge themselves on the rising nymphs, the floating duns, the egg-laying spinners, and the spent flies whose brief moment is ended. (The Latin name for May flies is *Ephemerida* which stems from the same root as our word *ephemeral*, meaning short-lived).

May flies may crawl about in the mud or among the stones and weeds of the stream bottom for as long as two years, but as winged insects they enjoy only a short spell of glory, sometimes but a few hours and at most a couple of days. Toward evening thousands of nymphs of the same species, as if by signal, rise to the stream or lake surface, float momentarily while the nymph shell splits down the back, then step out as winged May flies. After a short ride while the wings dry, these dull-colored duns fly ashore and rest again until they shed once more. This time they emerge bright and shiny and are known as spinners. The male spinners gather in a swarm over the water, each species with its own peculiar form of flight.

In a typical May fly dance, the male spinners fly directly up in the air for twenty or thirty feet, then drop back down again tail first, thousands of them making up a vast cloud of insects. The females fly out from the shore to join the males; then, with their heavy egg sacs, descend to the surface to spawn. Soon they drop to the water spent, with wings outspread, and it's all over.

Some species of May flies hatch, dance, and die the same evening. Others may go into their dance a day later, and the largest species waits until about forty-eight hours after hatching to return to the water from which they came.

The trout go crazy when there is so much insect food at hand, and at times the water surface fairly boils. The swifts and the swallows, and later the bats, get their share too. The only thing around the stream busier than these feeding fish and birds is the fisherman. He's frantically tying on new patterns of flies attempting to match the insect hatch . . . He knows that this magic hour is short . . . When he does finally succeed in choosing the correct fly, it is almost too dark to see it floating on the water . . . Then, it's all over: maybe he has landed a trout or two, and maybe he hasn't.

Dan Holland: TROUT FISHING, 1949.
(Thomas Y. Crowell Co., N. Y.)

DRY FLY ON THE MIRAMICHI

THERE WAS a difference of opinion at Burnt Hill camp. That was usually the case. The Doctor and I, with our guides, Don and Henry, and Earle, the cook, had been in camp for two weeks. The days had been spent in fishing, the evenings in discussing all the problems of the still mysterious salmon. The water had been at a good height, and of good color, the days comfortable; grilse were plenty and salmon in good number.

But there had come a change. The water had become not only low but crystal clear, and the days were insufferably hot. A blazing sun turned the surface of the calm "ponds" into a fierce glare, and the rapids were all a shimmering, glancing, dazzling foam at which it was painful to look. There seemed no use in fishing save at dawn and in the evening twilight, and even then for the last three days the most patient, the most skillful casting had failed to take a single fish. Not even a grilse had showed itself. For three days not a strike, not a rise.

And then the Doctor had had a happy thought. In the very low, clear water of the year before, some disappointed but adventurous angler on the Restigouche had experimented with the dry-fly. If dry-fly, in such conditions, would take trout when the wet-fly failed, why not salmon?

The unanimous opinion of us three had its usual effect. The Doctor was now resolved to try the dry-fly on the Miramichi. It was only midafternoon, but he proceeded at once to put his resolve into action. A large brown hackle was discovered among his trout-flies and carefully "doped"; a nine-foot dry-fly trout leader, his longest trout line and a six-ounce rod were selected, the line was greased, and the Doctor sallied forth. It would be ridiculous to try this tackle in the rapids or in the upper pond, whence the fish could make off at once, unchecked, down the main current of the rapids. But the wide lower pond, with its long sweep from the foot of the rapids to where it pitched over the lower falls, offered calmer and less obstructed water, with plenty of opportunity for the fish to run. So down to the lower pond went the Doctor, now flushed and eager. Don accompanied him with the gaff, an indulgent smile on his face that brought to my mind the biblical "Like as a father pitieth his children." Henry and I followed to scoff.

The Doctor and Don embarked in the canoe; Henry and I sat on the shore and grinned. Cast after cast flew out over the glassy water, the brown hackle floated serene and undisturbed, the canoe drifted almost imperceptibly down toward the lower pitch. And then—flash, bang, flurry, and a fish leaped into the air. A grilse of about three pounds. The hook was well set, the Doctor handled him skillfully, and in a few minutes the fish was in the boat. Only a grilse, but not so bad, an agreeable diversion in the monotony of fishless days.

Disappointed but encouraged, spurred by the ironical cheers of Henry and me, the Doctor flogged on. "It a grilse, why not a salmon?" In sleepy boredom, but just a little disturbed, a bit expectant with a wild surmise, Henry and I reclined on the bank. Don seemed nodding over his paddle. And then the waters parted and the miracle took place. There came a savage scuttering rush, the strike, the turn and off across the surface of the pond, making for the heavy current in the middle, went a great crazy salmon, slatting, tumbling, leaping again and again, the noise of the fish cloven by the strident, high-pitched shriek of the reel. With a simultaneous electric thrill Henry and I sat up and took notice.

Don was galvanized into life, the Doctor's face grew pale beneath the sunburn. Swiftly, swiftly out went the line from the little reel. Would he never stop? The line was down to the last few inches. Frantically Don dug in his paddle to follow. Of no avail to give him the butt of a six-ounce rod and break the paper-thin leader. Again the miracle. On the verge of escape he slowed, swerved, stopped. The canoe sped toward him, foot after foot of line was recovered. Then he was off again, but not in a flurry; steadily, determinedly, but slowly enough for Don to follow. Again a rush, again a great leap into the air, his head shaking savagely from side to side, and a tremendous splash as he fell back into the water.

It is needless to say that Henry and I from the moment of the strike had turned from scoff to prayer. We rooted for the Doctor in every fibre of our beings. I am ashamed to confess that in spite of long experience and habitual control of nerves, four men played that fish throughout the long fight. I doubt if the Doctor heard a word of the distilled wisdom that was so frantically hurled at him, but he must have been conscious of our windy sighs of relief as each critical moment was successfully overcome. And yet, we were all sure that ultimate disaster was inevitable. That little one-handed rod, reel within an inch or two of the end, no relief possible from the other hand or brace of rod against the body—how long could the Doctor's wrist hold out, how long before the leader must part under the strain?

The fish seemed no longer inclined to leap, but sullenly bored back and forth, constantly taking line that could be only painfully and slowly recovered. Slowly, skillfully, Don edged the canoe toward the shore, now losing his advantage, now regaining it inch by inch. At last the Doctor stood upon the shore, with firm ground beneath his feet and the opportunity to get below the fish and turn him whenever he made off toward the lower pitch and the snags and boulders that lay between. Shorter and shorter grew the turns of the fish, slower and slower the beat of his broad black tail. It seemed as if he would soon be coming to the gaff. But no! The salmon seemed to have caught his second wind. He was off again in a swift, long rush. The reel screamed; the barrel was almost bare of line.

Don is usually an unerring gaffer, never striking till the fish is in exactly the right position. To miss is an almost intolerable blow to his self-respect. But this time the strain of the long, impossible fight proved a little too much for his nerves; a little excess of anxiety to end it all deflected his aim—he struck and missed and the fish was off again. But he could not go far, he was really done for; and when he was brought in again, painfully, with the slightest possible strain, he came without a struggle, was gaffed like a piece of wood and deposited at our feet, with scarce a quiver left in him. And as he fell, the fly dropped from his mouth!

The Doctor sat down abruptly. He was pretty nearly as far gone as the fish. His left hand hung limp from a red, swollen wrist. For forty-five minutes it had borne the whole strain of the fight. Only the angler of long experience can estimate that strain, or the skill that had with that delicate tackle brought to grass that hard-fighting seventeen-pound salmon. Henry and I abased ourselves in the dust before him. We told him just what we thought of him, in the most superlative terms we could muster. There had never been so long, so difficult, so dangerous a fight; never had we beheld so nervy, so judgmatical, so expert an angler. Amid our enthusiasm, Don interjected now and then a laconic word of approbation—Don who had fished the Miramichi for fifty years; Don, prince of watermen and salmon-fisher unequaled.

George Bosworth Churchill: MIRAMICHI DAYS, 1924.
(Field & Stream Magazine)

DRY FLY FISHING

WHAT does dry-fly fishing mean?

Armed with a light rod, a fine cast, a single fly carefully selected, the exact counterpart of some insect that is or might be on the water, you carefully scan the stream. A "great old trout, both subtle and fearful" is seen to be on the feed in the narrow space between two beds of weed. Upstream you stalk him, crouching or crawling. More than a cast-length below the spot you pause, until again the ring of the rise is seen. A further cautious approach, a further kneeling wait when in position. Again the black nose appears, a fly is sucked down. The brain judges the distance to an inch, and simultaneously instructs the hand and eye. A preliminary cast is made across the stream, another wave of the rod, and the tiny fly alights jauntily on the water like a living thing—yet easily to be distinguished from the natural insects as the two move side by side. It floats lightly over the desired spot where lies the fish.

Half turning lazily on his side, lazily he opens his great white mouth and sucks in the fly, scarce dimpling the surface of the water the while.

A half-turn of the wrist and he is fast.

The reel makes merry music, while rapidly runs the line. Soon is the first rush over; cautiously the line is recovered, the fish appears to yield; another rush, again he yields; then, turning sharply, headlong he bolts downstream, for one anxious moment slackening the line. Another rush, a leap into the air, the strain is increased; he turns slightly on his side, but, quickly recovering himself, shakes his jaws; again he rolls, and again, at each roll showing more of his silvery side, and now like a log he lies motionless.

The right hand has grasped the landing-net, the left holds the rod with shortened line; the net sinks in the water, and, yielding to the gentle pressure, nearer he rolls; then, with a cautious, almost imperceptible movement, it is under him, and he lies gasping for breath upon the bank.

Lord Buxton: FISHING AND SHOOTING, 1902.
(John Murray, Ltd.)

ON THE COLOR OF FLIES

OUR first trip to Encampment (Wyoming) was made with Glenn Jones. He had been a correspondent for many years' standing so that when we decided to find out something about the Colorado country we asked Glenn about it and he responded not only by arranging the trip but by personally conducting it. He had previously been to Encampment and was so enthusiastic about it that he made it the principal objective of our itinerary, even though it wasn't in his beloved Colorado.

Glenn knew certain parts of this stretch of the Encampment well. He had had exceptional luck on some of the pools and naturally brought me to them first. There was one stretch to which he seemed very partial. It was quite a distance down in the Mica mine country near the entrance to the canyon. It was really the lower end of a shallow riffle where the formation of the bottom retarded the current and made a glide which spread out from bank to bank before concentrating into a solid volume of water which dashed down a short incline into the pool below. This pool wasn't much to brag about, as far as looks go. The bottom was mostly sand and the only cover was a few rocks at the point where the riffle above deepened and spread out into the basin.

This pool was Glenn's pet. He had made some really marvelous catches there. The first day we fished it he took one small Rainbow. I caught nothing. The next day Glenn took two Rainbows. I hooked and lost three. By this time we were in a bad frame of mind. The trout kept rising steadily and in a business-like manner but we couldn't take them.

The third day Glenn ignored the pool and went down into the canyon. Because the pool had aroused my curiosity I stopped there. As usual the trout were rising continually but I couldn't take any. I tired of it after a while and went down to the fast water below. Here the water was too fast to see many rises but occasionally I saw a dimple in a small eddy close to the opposite shore so knew that fish were working there. For an hour or more I concentrated on these fish, changing flies and sizes of flies until my patience was exhausted. Finally I tied on a No. 14 Adams—why I hadn't used this fly before is inexplicable—and the first time my fly floated over one of the tiny eddies a fish was hooked.

I lost this fish. It was a good one and a hard fighter. He rushed downstream and wound the leader around a rock. He succeeded in snagging it so badly that it was a case of either wading in and take a chance of spoiling the water for more fishing or losing most of it. I selected the latter alternative.

This incident upset me. To use a present-day word, I went "haywire." In five minutes I hooked as many fish and lost every one because of faulty playing. Everything I did was wrong. I held the fish so hard that they tore out. I forgot I had a reel and played them with loose line held in the hand which caused a break as soon as a fish made a long run. I didn't hold them hard enough and they wound the leader and line around the rocks. I did everything that one shouldn't do.

Fortunately, the loss of the sixth fish brought me to my senses. I suddenly realized that I wasn't in any state of mind to land fish that fought like these did. So I waded to shore where I sat and considered the inconsistency of anglers in general and the dumbness of one in particular. I smoked two cigarettes until they burned my fingers and finally I became tranquil.

This exercise of self-restraint did wonders. The first cast resulted in the landing of a seventeen-inch Rainbow. The next fish was a combination of an aerial acrobat, speedboat and submarine but I landed him. This was because I was coldly calculating and could gauge how much strain the 3X leader would take without breaking, could calmly anticipate the moves of the fish and sometimes forestall them.

After I had taken four of these scrappy trout, none of them under two pounds, I bethought myself of Glenn's pool. Perhaps this Adams would take them. So back I went. This time it was like taking candy from a baby. Every cast brought a rise and at least fifty per cent of the rises meant a hooked fish, all Rainbows going from 10 inches to two and three-quarters pounds.

"These grayish flies are the thing for Rainbows, all right," I exulted.

Then Glenn came along. He also had a good catch although he hadn't had as many rises as I. "What did you get them on?" I asked, fully expecting him to name some gray fly.

I was properly subdued when he replied: "The Royal Coachman!"

Ray Bergman: TROUT, 1949.
(Alfred A. Knoph, Inc.)

THE LAZY S CAST

IT WAS fall, the golden fall of the high North Park country of Colorado, with the quaking aspens running fingers of yellow gold up the ravines into the towering Continental Divide. Closer, the meandering North Platte was flanked with burnished gold cottonwoods and bronzed willows. Almost across the river from us, Steamer Brannon pointed out a tiny dimpling in the quiet backwater—no more disturbance really than might be made by a frost-chilled insect tumbling from the overhanging willows into the water. Then a couple of tattletale bubbles. "You take him, Gene," said Steamer, his voice needlessly dropping into a whisper.

Steamer did not know it, but he was about to witness a brand new cast—after I had made a conventional cast.

Even with wading, sixty-five feet remained to the spot where I had to drop my favorite No. 16, Gantron-dressed, full-palmered Light Caddis artificial fly. Before casting, I honed the point of my small hook needle-sharp, and tested my 12-foot tapered leader moistening the tippet by drawing it through my mouth. "Only large trout," warned Steamer, "make such tiny sucking dimples on the North Platte."

I got my conventional cast off nicely and my fly rode high and dry over the still-working trout. We watched intently as it floated a few inches, then a foot. As it went over the feeding fish, Steamer said fervently: "If that float doesn't take him, Gene, nothing will." It floated on, another foot. Two feet. I was still set for the swirl of the trout when my fly dragged out, leaving a tell-tale wake pulled out by the current which had bellied my line mid-stream. As I retrieved my fly slowly, I noted happily that I had not put down the fish. The tiny dimples kept coming in the same spot.

With the conventional cast behind me, I was now set to see if I could take the same trout with my simple new cast which might well eliminate a lot of complicated casts now used by anglers to get that prized independent dry fly float.

I began the cast like any other, but as my double-tapered line looped forward overhead, I waggled my rod sideways a half dozen times and this imparted a series of Lazy SSSSes into my line and these in turn dropped on the water between me and the fly which settled, almost inch for inch, where it had before with my conventional cast. (Lazy S is a western branding term, meaning that the S lies, lazy-like, on its side).

But this time, something wonderful happened. Although resting on the same water, my fly didn't move! Surprised, Steamer exclaimed: "What's the matter with your fly, Gene? It isn't moving."

"It's my new cast," I explained while watching the fly intently. "You see, I build a lot of Lazy SSSSes into my line and while the main current of the river washes them out, my fly rests independently on the quiet water just as a dead insect might."

Certainly, the behavior of my fly was in sharp contrast to my previous float when my fly moved slowly—pulled by the line, however perfect the float had seemed to Steamer Brannon, although it had not deceived the trout.

My reward was not lacking. Just as Steamer said: "Well, I'll be damned! I thought your first float was perfect!" my Caddis quietly disappeared—sucked under with a hardly-perceptible dimple. I struck and was fast to a solid fish. He fought gamely as would any self-respecting deep-bellied four-teen-inch brown in spring-cold water.

There are two drawbacks to the Lazy S but once they are recognized and mastered they become blessings in disguise. First, the loose SSSSes put a great deal of slack in the line so that when a fish rises, the angler must transmit his strike through this slack. Fortunately, with a good floating line the impact of the angler's strike travels readily along the SSSSes. And if the angler uses a needle-point sharp hook, it is not necessary to move the fly more than a quarter inch to sink it beyond the barb.

This is the blessing: with all the slack line out, the angler simply cannot strike his fish so hard and with the softer imposed strike he can use a finer and less visible leader without danger of parting it on the strike— and losing his fish. Where before he needed a 3X tippet, now he can use a 4X successfully. And the finer the leader, the easier it is to fool the sagacious large trout! To my sorrow, however, I found that I could not step down two grades from 3X to 5X and lost three good fish on the Williamson in Oregon before I returned to 4X.

The second drawback is that the angler's strike is slowed up. By using the Lazy S, the angler will find himself adding more distance to his cast because for the first time he will be able to get a perfect float in water which is farther away—and often in big trout water, happily, which has remained comparatively unmolested or poorly-covered by other fly fisher-men. Due to the longer cast, and the SSSSes, the impulse of his strike is transmitted farther and hence more slowly.

The blessing? With big trout, this delay is good. Most dry fly men take the fly away from their big fish—particularly the brown and eastern brook who are very deliberate when they grow up and get big. I have yet to see the dry fly angler who is too slow on large trout.

Once the basic rudiments of the Lazy S are mastered, and this can be done during a weekend's trouting, every angler will find himself experimenting with adaptations. By timing the waggle of the rod as the tapered line loops forward, the angler can build in his lazy SSSSes into practically any section of the line he desires, depending upon where the fast intervening water runs—either toward the fly or toward the butt of the line near the rod tip. It can also be used effectively with a roll cast. As the point of the line loops over, let the line slide through the guides and waggle the rod sharply.

The Lazy S works well in upstream fishing, too. Using it for the first time on the Gallatin in Montana, I got the rudest shock of my fishing life. I had thought, as I presume most dry fly anglers do, that I could wade and cast upstream, quartering if necessary, and with a slight hook cast get well-nigh perfect trout-deceiving floats. How wrong can a fisherman be? I found that by gently waggling in some elongated SSSSes into my line, as the fly floated toward me, that the S nearest me straightened out first and the fly floated toward me much more slowly than did the butt of my line. The deduction was inescapable: even in fishing these seemingly evenly-flowing currents, my fly had dragged imperceptibly.

Certainly I should have known better. After all, the uneven floor of the stream, the changes in width of the confining banks, the submerged rocks, the weeds, roots, gravel, sand—everything conspired to set up varying amounts of friction in the water—either holding it, blocking it, or speeding it on, producing a coiling, rushing, twisting uneven front going downstream with the seemingly smooth current. And the more conflicting the current, the more satisfaction does this controlled Lazy S cast give the angler.

With use, the angler will soon sense when he needs large SSSSes or small sssses. Essentially, it is a matter of "reading" the intensity of the conflicting currents and the angle used in quartering the stream. Customarily, upstreamwards the SSSSes should be smaller; across-streamwards, larger.

Larger SSSSes can be made by throwing a larger loop in the line—bringing the line forward more softly and waggling the rod more vigorously and letting the line slip through the guides, while the smaller sssses can be had by casting the line in a tighter loop and waggling the rod more gently.

The proof of the Lazy S's effectiveness depends upon one thing: Does it put more fish on the end of the line?

Upon numerous occasions when I have reverted to the conventional casts—as I did that fall day with Steamer Brannon on the North Platte, I have cast to rising fish without effect. Then, by casting to the same fish with the same fly my Lazy S has raised them. This I have done not just once, but a hundred times—often enough, to convince my many fishing companions on a dozen streams across the country that the Lazy S—simple as it is, can be made one of the most significant casts in a dry fly man's repertoire.

Eugene Burns, 1952.

THE ECSTASY OF THE WET FLY

THERE are those who wax indignant at the use of the wet-fly on dry-fly waters. Yet it has a special fascination. The indications which tell your dry-fly angler when to strike are clear and unmistakable, but those which bid a wet-fly man raise his rod-point and draw in the steel are frequently so subtle, so evanescent and impalpable to the senses, that, when the bending rod assures him that he has divined aright, he feels an ecstasy as though he had performed a miracle each time.

G. E. M. Skues: MINOR TACTICS OF THE CHALK-STREAM, 1910.
(A. and C. Black Ltd.)

THE CHIEF PLEASURE

THE Trout makes the angler the most gentlemanly and readiest sport of all other fishes: if you angle with a made fly, and a line twice your rod's length or more, of three hairs, in a plain water without wood, in a dark windy day from midafternoon, and have learned the cast of the fly.

If the wind be rough, and trouble the crust of the water, he will take it in the plain deeps, and then and there commonly the greatest may rise. When you have hooked him, give him leave! keeping your line straight. Hold him from the roots, and he will tire himself. This is the chief pleasure of Angling.

William Lauson: notes to SECRETS OF ANGLING, 1613.
(Editor of John Dennys' Secrets of Angling).

SALMON ON WHITE FLY

I HAVE said that there is no animal in nature resembling our salmon flies; but I once caught a fish who was certainly persuaded that he was attacking an animal that he had previously seen flying. This event happened when I was a novice.

Walter Ronaldson was attending me, and we were walking by the side of the Elm-wheel in the Pavilion-water. Walter was some way in advance, when I saw a white butterfly fluttering up and down over the water, and a salmon make a fruitless dart at it. It chanced that I had made some large salmon flies with white wings, in imitation of a pattern that was formerly the fashion for trout fishing, and was called, I know not why, the coachman. One of these I immediately looped to my line; the fish, no doubt taking it for the butterfly that he saw flitting above him, came at it at once, and I took him.

When he was landed, Walter's astonishment was great when he saw the fly, and he made a dozen imitations of it before he laid his head on the pillow. I should not think that under other circumstances such a fly would be alluring.

William Scrope: DAYS AND NIGHTS OF SALMON-FISHING, 1843.
(James Blackwood & Co., Ltd.)

THE ATTRACTIVENESS OF A FLY

I WOULD arrange the factors governing the attractiveness of a fly in the following order of relative importance:
1. The light-effects of the fly, above and below the surface.
2. The way the fly is cast and manipulated, including where the fly is placed relative to the fish.
3. Visibility of the leader to the fish.
4. The size of the fly.
5. Design of the fly.
6. Color of the fly.
7. Accuracy of imitation of natural insects.

It was not until I began to realize the relative importance of these factors that I became a real fisherman. By that I mean one who takes fish on a fly when others fail.

Edward Ringwood Hewitt:
A TROUT AND SALMON FISHERMAN FOR SEVENTY-FIVE YEARS, 1950.
(Charles Scribner's Sons, N. Y.)

FISH FEED EXCEEDINGLY ON SUCH YOUNG FLIES

I HAVE often observed and beheld in a sunshine day, in shallow waters, especially where any dung or fatte earth is therewith mingled: I say, I have seene a young flie swimme in the water too and fro, and in the end come to the upper crust of the water, and assay to flie up: howbeit not being perfectly ripe or fledge, hath twice or thrice fallen downe againe into the water; howbeit in the end receiving perfection by the heate of the sunne and the pleasant fat water, hath in the end within some halfe houre after taken her flight, and flied quite awaie into the ayre.

And of such young flies before they are able to flie awaie, do fish feed exceedingly.

John Taverner:

CERTAINE EXPERIMENTS CONCERNING FISH AND FRUITE, 1600.

Companionship

BROTHER OF THE ANGLE

I WOULD you were a brother of the angle; for a companion that is cheerful, and free from swearing and scurrilous discourse, is worth gold. I love such mirth as does not make friends ashamed to look upon one another next morning; nor men that cannot well bear it, to repent the money they spent when they be warmed with drink.

And take this for a rule, you may pick out such times, and such companies, that you may make yourselves merrier for a little than a great deal of money; for "'Tis the company and not the charge that makes the feast;" and such a companion you prove: I thank you for it.

Izaak Walton: THE COMPLEAT ANGLER, 1653.

THESE OBLIGING LITTLE HUMOURS

As I was yesterday morning walking with Sir Roger before his house, a country-fellow brought him a huge fish, which, he told him, Mr. *William Wimble* had caught that very morning; and that he presented it with his service to him, and intended to come and dine with him. At the same time he delivered a letter, which my friend read to me as soon as the messenger left him.

"*Sir Roger,*

I desire you to accept of a jack, which is the best I have caught this season, I intend to come and stay with you a week, and see how the perch bite in the *Black River*. I observed with some concern, the last time I saw you upon the bowling-green, that your whip wanted lash to it; I will bring half a dozen with me that I twisted last week, which I hope will serve you all the time you are in the country. I have not been out of the saddle for six days last past, having been at *Eton* with Sir *John's* eldest son. He takes to his learning hugely.

I am, Sir,

Your humble servant,

Will Wimble."

This extraordinary letter, and message that accompanied it, made me very curious to know the character and quality of the gentleman who sent them, which I found to be as follow:

Will Wimble is younger brother to a baronet, and descended of the ancient family of the *Wimbles*. He is now between forty and fifty; but being bred to no business and born to no estate, he generally lives with his elder brother as superintendent of his game.

He hunts a pack of dogs better than any man in the country, and is very famous for finding out a hare. He is extremely well versed in all the little handicrafts of an idle man; he makes a *Mayfly* to a miracle; and furnishes the whole country with anglerods.

As he is a good-natur'd officious fellow, and very much esteem'd upon account of his family, he is a welcome guest at every house, and keeps up a good correspondence among all the gentlemen about him. He carries a tulip-root in his pocket from one to another, or exchanges a puppy between a couple of friends that live perhaps in the opposite sides of the country. *Will* is a particular favourite of all the young heirs, whom he frequently obliges with a net that he has weaved, or a setting-dog that he has *made* himself. He now and then presents a pair of garters of his own knitting to their mothers or sisters, and raises a great deal of mirth among them by enquiring as often as he meets them *how they wear!*

These gentleman-like manufactures and obliging little humours make *Will* the darling of the country.

Joseph Addison, 1672-1719: THE SPECTATOR, NO. 108.

A MAN WORTH KNOWING

ON A chilly afternoon in late April, we were driving along Route 17 of New York state. The day had been devoted mainly to exploration. As we approached Cook's Falls, we saw two cars parked on the bank of the Beaverkill beside the Island Pool. Four fishermen stood at the edge of the road, chatting and having a round of steaming coffee from a generous thermos jug. We waved a greeting and would have passed had my eye not caught a glimpse of some fish on the running board of one of the cars. Hastily I stopped my car and threw the gears into reverse.

My friend and I stood before that catch of trout and gazed at them, speechless with envy and admiration. Seven fish, the smallest fifteen inches and the largest twenty-one! They had been neatly arranged according to size, and all were fresh-caught and glistening in the fading light of the April afternoon.

"Nice, ain't they?" said a voice behind us.

"Nice!" I repeated. "They're magnificent." I turned to look at the speaker. "Do you mind," I asked him, "telling me what fly you took them on?"

"Mind?" he said, smiling. "Certainly not. It's no secret. We got 'em on Quill Gordons, number twelve, dry."

That was the first time I had seen John Burns. Short, stocky, and with a genial smile on his round face, he fairly radiated health and good cheer. In later years I came to know him well, and my first estimate of him as a man worth knowing was never changed.

"Mister," I said earnestly, "I'd give a lot for the privilege of watching you fish one of these days."

John threw back his head and laughed. Then he stopped suddenly and regarded me intently.

"Have you got your tackle and waders with you?" he asked.

"Right there in the car," I replied.

"No time like the present," he said. "Hurry and get rigged up. The rise is about over, but maybe we can pick up a couple."

John Burns died about ten years later. During that ten years I was lucky enough to spend many days with him on the lower waters of his beloved Beaverkill. From him I learned the unusual and less obvious things of the woods and streams. It is my hope that he now casts his Quill Gordon, No. 12, dry, on the crystal-clear waters of the streams that flow down the other slope of the great divide. Thinking about him, I can hear him reply to the Angel Gabriel's query of "What luck?" "Not so good today, Gabe. Only a couple. But, say—ain't it fun?"

John Alden Knight:

THE THEORY AND TECHNIQUE OF FRESH WATER ANGLING, 1945.
(Harcourt, Brace & Co., Inc., N. Y.

WE DRINK SWEET HEALTHS

When homeward from the streams we turn
Good cheer our sport replaces,
There's liquor twinkling in the glass,
There's joy on all our faces!

We drink sweet healths, a merry round,
We talk old stories over,
And sing glad staves, like summer birds
Below their leafy cover.

Thus cheerily our evenings pass,
Till lulled below the quilting
We sleep our toils off, and are forth
Before the lark is lilting.

All joy be with our hearts' kin bold!
May care's nets ne'er entangle,
Nor woe nor poverty depress
A brother of the angle!

Thomas Tod Stoddart: ANGLING SONGS, 1866.
(James Blackwood & Co., Ltd.)

TO ANDREW LANG

Dear Andrew, with the brindled hair,
Who glory to have thrown in air,
High over arm, the trembling reed,
By Ale and Kail, by Till and Tweed:
An equal craft of hand you show
The pen to guide, the fly to throw:
I count you happy starred; for God,
When he with inkpot and with rod
Endowed you, bade your fortune lead
For ever by the crooks of Tweed,
For ever by the woods of song
And lands that to the Muse belong;
Or if in peopled streets, or in
The abhorred pedantic sanhedrin,
It should be yours to wander, still
Airs of the morn, airs of the hill,
The plovery Forest and the seas
That break about the Hebrides,
Should follow over field and plain
And find you at the window pane;
And you again see hill and peel,
And the bright springs gush at your heel.
So went the fiat forth, and so
Garrulous like a brook you go,
With sound of happy mirth and sheen
Of daylight—whether by the green
You fare that moment, or the gray;
Whether you dwell in March or May;
Or whether treat of reels and rods
Or of the old unhappy gods:
Still like a brook your page has shone,
And your ink sings of Helicon.

Robert Louis Stevenson, 1850-1894.
(The Society of Authors)

WALTON, SAGE BENIGN

While flowing rivers yield a blameless sport,
  Shall live the name of Walton: Sage benign!
  Whose pen the mysteries of the rod and line
    Unfolding, did not fruitless by exhort
To reverend watching of each still report
  That Nature utters from her rural shrine.
  Meek, nobly versed in simple discipline—
He found the longest summer day too short,
  To his loved pastime given by sedgy Lee,
Or down the tempting maze of Shawford brook—
Fairer than life itself, in this sweet Book,
  The cowslip-bank and shady willow tree;
And the fresh meads—where flowed, from every nook
  Of his full bosom, gladsome Piety!

William Wordsworth, 1770-1850: Written On a Blank Leaf in "THE COMPLEAT ANGLER."

TO MASTER IZAAK WALTON

Master, I trow 'tis many a year
Since last you fared a-fishing here,
Since first you cast your eager flies
Athwart the streams of Paradise.
And we, we love to read thy book
By placid stream and trickling brook,
When trout are scarce or winds are loud,
Or when the sky hath never a cloud.
But you are in a happier mead,
Where fish are ever on the feed.

And, master, these are evil days
When scarce a man our art may praise.
For some they say 'tis most unfit
For bearded men in peace to sit,
And watch a meditative hook,

102

COMPANIONSHIP

Or read a cheerful, pleasant book,
When they should to their work be hieing,
For time is short and all are dying.
And some they hold 'tis most unkind
Around the hook the silk to wind,
And hold a fish with barb of steel—
As if, forsooth, a fish could feel.

But some there were both stout and hale
Who did not bow the knee to Baal.
Good Master Stoddart, now with God,
Full well he loved to walk the sod
On a fresh, westering April day
And see the sportive salmon play.

And the great singer of the north,
He loved by stream to wander forth;
He hated not the rod and line,
He called thee "Walton, sage, benign."
And some there be in London town,
Of bookish men, who often down
To the green country come to try
Their long-loved skill of fishery.

Why weary thee with idle praise,
Thou wanderer in Elysian ways?
Where skies are fresh and fields are green,
And never dust nor smoke is seen,
Nor news sheets, nor subscription-lists,
Nor merchants, nor philanthropists.
For there the waters fall and flow
By fragrant banks, and still below
The great three-pounders rise and take
The "palmer," "alder," "dun," or "drake."
Now by that stream, if there you be,
I prithee keep a place for me.

Lord Tweedsmuir (John Buchan): MUSA PISCATRIX, 1896.
(John Lane The Bodley Head, Ltd.)

A MAN WITH WHOM I HAVE OFTEN FISHED

THAT under-valuer of money, the late Provost of Eton College, Sir Henry Wotton—a man with whom I have often fished and conversed, a man whose foreign employments in the service of this nation, and whose experience, learning, wit, and cheerfulness made his company to be esteemed one of the delights of mankind: this man, whose very approbation of Angling were sufficient to convince any modest censurer of it, this man was also a most dear lover, and a frequent practiser of the art of Angling; of which he would say, "'Twas an employment for his idle time, which was then not idly spent," for Angling was, after tedious study, "a rest to his mind, a cheerer of his spirits, a diverter of sadness, a calmer of unquiet thoughts, a moderator of passions, a procurer of contendedness:" and "that it begat habits of peace and patience in those that professed and practised it."

Indeed, my friend, you will find Angling to be like the virtue of humility, which has a calmness of spirit, and a world of other blessings attending upon it. Sir, this was the saying of that learned man.

Izaak Walton: THE COMPLEAT ANGLER, 1653.

Tall Tales

THE BET

"You are looking at that old creel with the bottom out. Ha, ha! That was a good joke. Jack Whirter and I had a bet of a dinner who would kill the biggest weight of fish one day, when we were in Sutherlandshire, on the ————. Jack was a smart hand—a very smart hand—and, while I was fishing the main river, Jack came upon a small brook that had spated from a night's rain, and, chancing on some worms, he went up the brook, and made a great take by a great fluke, while I, fishing in the main river lower down, had a fair basket, but nothing extra—Jack came home beaming. The trap was to call for us at a certain bridge, and take us back to dinner.

While on the bridge waiting, I wanted to weigh Jack's take, but he would not allow me, wishing to do the triumphant when he arrived at the inn. Very good! The trap came up, and we got in, with Jones and Crawfull, who

105

had been fishing higher up; but there was no room for our creels inside, so we strapped them on the hinder rail.

Now master Jack was a wee bit of a skinflint; his soul loved cheap lines, and he would put up with any amount of tangling and inconvenience rather than pay a good price for a good thing. Cheap flies at 1s. 6d. a dozen he also adored, no matter how the hooks broke or the tying came to pieces. His waders were always patched to a marvel, and his creel was a caution. Yet Jack Whirter was a city swell, and with thousands a year.

As we jogged home, I had my arm over the back of the trap, and, most inadvertently, my hand embraced the bottom of Jack Whirter's creel, and I felt the head of a trout nearly protruding through a broken spar in the basket-work, and, as I was fumbling about it curiously, the trout (quite a small one) oozed through and dropped in the road.

Had I lost my bet? Ha! an idea seized me. He wouldn't weigh at the bridge! So I gently detached another spar of the basket-work, and then I looked up at the stars with an angelic smile, and took them into my confidence, and we winked at one another as we heard a soft flop on the dusty road behind every now and then.

When we got home, after the usual questions and answers, "How stands the bet?" was the cry.

"Oh, that I won, of course!" said Whirter.

"Well, I don't know about 'of course'," I said, "But we'll settle that point by weighing in."

"All right," said Jack, and out he went to fetch his creel. I brought mine in with me, and the scales were got ready for the match.

"Halloo!" we heard from the doorway; "Halloo! Why what's this? My creel is as light as a feather!" and in came Jack with an empty creel in his hand—at least, there was only one small trout left in it—and with half the bottom out. There was a roar at that, I tell you, Jack stood, looking like a fool, while Jones, an aggravating chap, said: "Ah, I always told you that those cheap creels were not to be trusted!"

"Cheap! Why it's worn out ages ago," said Crawfull, fingering the bottom.

"Well, let's weigh in," said I, innocently.

Jack had to pay for the dinner, and it was years before I told him the whole joke, but by that time he had improved somewhat, and that is the basket.

Francis Francis: HOT POT; OR MISCELLANEOUS PAPERS, 1880.
(The Field Magazine)

HAS YE BEEN SWALLERED?

—(Noah an' Jonah an' Cap'n John Smith,
Fisherman an' travelers, narreratin' myth,
Settin' up in Heaven all eternity,
Fishin' in the shade, contented as could be!
Spittin' their terbaccer in the little shaded creek,
Stoppin' of their yarns fer ter hear the ripples speak!
I hope fer Heaven, when I think of this—
You folks bound hellward, a lot of fun you'll miss!)

Jonah, he decapitates that mudcat's head,
An' gets his pipe ter drawin'; an' this is what he said:
"Excuse me ef your stories don't excite me much!
Excuse me ef I seldom agitate fer such!
YOU think yer fishermen! I won't argue none!
I won't even tell yer the half o' what I done!
You has careers dangerous an' checkered!
All as I will say is: Go and read my record!
You think yer fishermen! You think yer great!
All I asks is this: Has one of ye been 'BAIT'?
Cap'n Noah, Cap'n John, I heerd when ye hollered;
What I asks is this: Has one of ye been SWALLERED?
It's mighty purty fishin' with little hooks an' reels.
It's mighty easy fishin' with little rods an' creels.
It's mighty pleasant ketchin' mudcats fer yer dinners.
But this here is my challenge fer saints an' fer sinners,
Which one of ye v'yaged in a vermint's inners?
When I seen a big fish, tough as Methooslum,
I used for to dive into his oozly-goozlum!
When I seen the strong fish, wallopin' like a lummicks,
I useter foller 'em, dive into their stummicks!
I could v'yage an' steer 'em, I could understand 'em,
I useter navigate 'em, I useter land 'em!
Don't you pester ME with any more narration!
Go git famous! Git a reputation!"

Don Marquis: NOAH AN' JONAH AN' CAP'N JOHN SMITH, 1921.
(Appleton-Century-Crofts, Inc. N. Y.)

TO BOB FOR WHALE

For angling-rod he took a sturdy oake;
For line, a cable that in storm ne'er broke;
His hooke was such as heads the end of pole
To pluck down house ere fire consumes it whole;
The hook was baited with a dragon's tale,—
And then on rock he stood to bob for whale.

Sir William D'Avenant: BRITANNIA TRIUMPHANS, 1637.

OUR BIGGEST FISH

I never lost a little fish—
Yes, I am free to say.
It always was the biggest fish
I caught, that got away.

Eugene Field, 1850-1895.
(Charles Scribner's Sons, N. Y.)

ANTONY FISHES WITH CLEOPATRA

CLEOPATRA: *Give me mine angle, we'll to th' river; there,*
My music, playing far off, I will betray
Tawny-finn'd fishes; my bended hook shall pierce
Their slimy jaws, and as I draw them up
I'll think them every one an Antony,
And say, Ah, ha! you're caught!

CHARMIAN: *'Twas merry when*
You wagere'd on your angling; when your diver
Did hang a salt-fish on his hook, which he
With fervency drew up!

William Shakespeare: ANTHONY AND CLEOPATRA, 1606.

108

LITTLE FISHES TALK

IF YOU were to make little fishes talk, they would talk like whales.

James Boswell, 1740-1795. LIFE OF DR. JOHNSON.
(Oliver Goldsmith to Samuel Johnson).

DUCK AND EEL

FOR eels and wild ducks, put hooks upon warp or line, about a foot apart, and the same length to each hook; put a gudgeon on one hook, and a piece of lights on the other all the way: lay it across the shallow waters. The lights will swim, which the ducks will take, and the eels will take the gudgeons; so when, you draw the line out, you will have a duck on one hook, and an eel on the other. This you will find to be excellent sport.

John Mayer: THE SPORTSMAN'S DIRECTORY, 1823.

OULD SALVESTYR

"WHAT's Salvestyr?' says he.

"Salvestyr," says I, "Is a great salmon; some say he's twenty, some thirty, some forty pounds, that lies in the hole where your honour killed the trout on Tuesday; and he's always rising and sometimes takes, but no one was able to kill him,—yet he snapped the rod out of Ned Bryan's hand last Sunday night, and broke it between the stones, so that Ned never got as much of it as would make a toothpick for a lamper eel, and *that* lives by suction like the snipes."

" 'Well,' says he to me, 'if thou wilt tie the flies, I will go with thee in the morning: at what hour wilt thou be ready?'

" 'Oh, de dad,' says I, 'In the grey dawn just before the sun rises, and that'll be about half past three; I'll be under your honour's windy.'

"Well, Dinny Considine and myself brought him to the ould spot, and I gev him an oul Lochaber, that I had killed a dozen peal with, and we tould him the only way to fish the pool was to drag it; so we made him let out about twenty yards o' line, and sit with his face to the stern,—and God

109

knows I was glad o' that, for I couldn't look at him without laughin', and his back was to me, and I was making faces at Dinny. By and by we seen he was getting tired and fidgety; and Dinny, with a turn o' the paddle, put the fly in a stone, and snapt it off clean as a whistle.

" 'Your honour hooked him,' says I.

" 'Verily,' says he, 'I felt a strong pull, and thou must have heard the noise of the reel.'

" 'I did,' says I, 'I knew you were in him; but we'd better look at the fly.'

"With that he wound up, and there sure enough was the hook bruk in two.

" 'Oh the thief of the world,' says Dinny. 'It was Salvestyr was at it, and he'll rise again; but give him a bigger fly, he thinks nothing of a dozen of them little ones.'

"With that I takes out of me hat a great spring fly on thribble gut, and I says, 'If he sucks in *that,* it'll hould him, or the divil won't hould him;' and I spit on it for luck, and threw it into the wather, and at it we went again, dragging the hole over and hether, until we were getting towards the tail of it where the big log of bog yew is lying on the bottom, when I tips Dinny the wink, and we let the cot drop sudden a bit down with the stream, and then gave her a smart pull up again, when the hook struck as fast in the log as the rock of Cashel. The Quaker's reel called out 'Murder,' and we, letting the cot run *down* with the stream, the ould Ommadhawn thought Salvestyr was runing *up* it.

"Dinny cries out: "Butt him your honour '

"I was near falling into the wather with the laughin', but I threw down the oar and tuk up the pole, and stopped the cot, and cried out: 'Now your Soul, wind on him.'

"With that the old Quaker began winding on his reel as if he was grinding coffee for the bare life, and we quietly poled the cot up towards the log until we got fair over it.

" 'Now,' says I, 'feel him, surr, see if you can left him;' with that he bent the rod till I thought either it or his back would break.

" 'Ah, the oul divil,' says Dinny, 'He's gone to the bottom to sulk; but be ready for him, Surr, he'll take another race, and then may be we'll put the gaff in him.' With that Dinny takes his pole off the ground, and down goes the cot like winkin: the Quaker thinking it was the fish was going up, and sweating, saving your presence, till he looked like ould Neptune in Lord Clare's fountain. Down again the Quaker took to winding up, and we got over the log, and Dinny cries out: 'I see him! Ages! What a fish he is, he's as big as a horse,—give me the gaff!'

"With that he made believe to make a blow of the gaff at him.

" 'Put me a little to the right,' says he, and I give the cot a short turn round, and down went the Quaker on his face and hands, but he held on to the rod as if it was his pocket-book; but the cot was running down the stream, and just as he got on his legs again all his line was run off the reel, and Salvestyr carried line, gut and fly clean and clear away.

"Oh, ye'r Honour, if you'd seen how blank he looked, as if I was going to scold him; but he ped for the line and fly like an ould gentleman, which you know he was not; and Dinny and myself had a good laugh when we went in the evening to take the fly out of Salvestyr, and gather up the line from the bottom."

William Agar Adamson: SALMON-FISHING IN CANADA, 1860.
(Longmans Green & Co., Ltd.)

Night Fishing

A BASS TO MOUNT

THE telephone rang and the cheerful voice on the other end of the line was that of Alex Sweigart, editor of the *Pennsylvania Angler*. He said that his friend, Baird Hershey, taxidermist at the state museum, wished to secure a big bass for mounting. Strangely, there was no such thing in the state collection. It would be a hand-painted papier mache mount made from a mold and it would be done in duplicate so that the man who supplied the fish would be the recipient of a reproduction. It was a Friday afternoon and Alex was advising some of the fellows of this request, he said, in the hope that a suitable fish would be produced promptly. Here was a challenge and an interesting sort of proposition.

I knew where there were two fine bass in a rather small ledge pocket either of which would qualify as a fine museum specimen. A heat wave accompanied by drought was in progress, so it seemed advisable to concentrate on night fishing.

About nine-thirty Saturday evening I slipped into casting position. Distant flashes of heat lightning periodically illuminated the stream so that it was

113

possible to obtain quick glimpses of the protruding ledge that was directly below the pocket where I had seen these fish the previous week. From my position to the side and slightly above the pocket, the Baby Popper could be cast into the hole, a distance of about eighty feet, and fished slightly against the current thus producing the best possible popping action and noise. The lure had been especially equipped with bronze hooks so that if a strike was forthcoming from one of those fish, I would have the best possible chance of sinking the hooks.

The light spat of the lure and the popping sound that followed were just right. As the lure passed over the best part of the water, there were successive flashes of lightning. Nothing happened. The sky remained dark during the progress of the next retrieve.

There is great tension when one is concentrating on his angling and doing the best he can over the known position of a fine fish.

Suddenly anticipation was substantiated by a noisy eruption of the water in the darkness of the night. I snapped the rod upward and it arched and throbbed in response to a heavy live weight. The fight that ensued was rough and noisy before a tired bass was slid out of the water on a sand bar. When I placed my hand on it in the darkness and felt the broad side, I knew I had one well over four pounds; three and three-quarters pounds would not have been enough; anything over four pounds was satisfactory. Elated, I turned homeward with pleasant thoughts in mind.

I arrived at the museum Monday morning with my prize carefully wrapped in a wet towel. As I approached the workshop, I could see a group of people among whom were Alex Sweigart, Baird Hershey the taxidermist, and Lloyd King. They were in a huddle apparently examining something. As I approached, Alex jubilantly proclaimed: "Look at this; Lloyd brought in a bass for Baird."

Before them was a real one, all twenty-two inches, five pounds ten ounces of him! It came from the Juniata river taken at dusk on a Jitter Bug. Lloyd explained that he had previously located the fish and he had taken it exactly where he figured it to be.

Alex noticed something under my arm. "What's that?" he enquired.

"Oh, just a package," I casually replied and turned to leave.

"They don't wrap things in towels," and with that he relieved me of my burden. By comparison, of course my fish was insignificant.

Charles K. Fox: ADVANCED BAIT CASTING, 1950.
(G. P. Putnam's Sons, N. Y.)

RASCALLY FELLOWS

IN THE NIGHT usually the best Trouts bite, and will rise ordinarily in the still deeps; but not so well in the Streams. And although the best and largest Trouts bite in the Night (being afraid to stir, or range about in the Day time), yet I account this way of Angling both unwholsum, unpleasant, and very ungentiel, and to be used by none but Idle pouching Fellows.

Therefore I shall say nothing of it, only describe how to lay Night Hooks; which, if you live close by a River side, or have a large Moat, or Pond at your own House, will not be unpleasant, sometimes to practise.

But as for Damming, Groping, Spearing, Hanging, Twitcheling, Netting, or Firing by Night, I purposely omit them, and them esteem to be used only by disorderly and rascally Fellows.

James Chetham: THE ANGLER'S VADE MECUM, 1681.

FISH FOR BREAKFAST

MY LORD sent to me at Sun going down to provide him a good dish of trouts against the next morning by sixe of the clock. I went to the door to see how the wanes of the aire were like to prove. I returned answer, that I doubted not, God willing, but to be provided at his time appointed.

I went presently to the river, and it proved very dark; I drew out a line of three silks and three hairs twisted for the uppermost part, and a line of two hairs and two silks twisted for the lower part, with a good large hook; I baited my hook with two lob-worms, the four ends hanging as meet as I could guess them in the dark; I fell to angle. It proved very dark, so that I had good sport angling with the lob-worms as I do with the flye on the top of the water; you shall hear the fish rise at the top of the water, then you must loose a slack line down to the bottom as nigh as you can guess, then hold your line straight, feeling the fish bite, give time, there is no doubt of losing the fish, for there is not one among twenty but doth gorge the bait; the least stroke you can strike fastens the hook and makes the fish sure; letting the fish take a turn or two, you may take the fish up with your hands.

The night began to alter and grow somewhat lighter, I took off the lob-worms and set to my rod a white Palmer-flye, made of a large hook; I had sport for the time until it grew lighter; so I took off the white Palmer and set to a red Palmer made of a large hook; I had good sport until it grew very light. Then I took off the red Palmer and set to a black Palmer; I had good sport, made up the dish of fish.

So I put up my tackles and was with my Lord at his time appointed for the service.

Thomas Barker: BARKER'S DELIGHT, 1657.

Fishing Tackle

THE IMPLEMENTS APPERTAYNING

IN AS MUCH as the first ground Worke or Substance of this Art of Angling consisteth in the implements belonging and appertayning thereunto, and that except a man be possest of them which are most exact, nimble or necessary for the same, his labour is vayne, and to little or no purpose imployed, and for as much as the Angle-rod is the greatest, principallest, and sole direct or of all other Tooles belonging thereunto, I think it not amisse to begin with the choyse and order thereof, according to the opinions of the best noted Anglers, which either have bin in times past, or at this day living.

For the choyce then of your Angle-Rod you shall understand that some Anglers are of opinion, that the best should be composed of two peeces, a

117

maine body, and a small plieant top. The maine body would be of a fine growne ground-witchen, or a ground Elme, of at least nine or ten foote in length, straight, smooth, without knots, and not much differing at either end in one substance or thicknesse.

The

Angle

Rod

It would be gathered at the fall of the leafe, neere; Or about Al hallontide, and layd up in some dry place, where it may lie straight, and of itselfe season: For to bake them in the fire (as many do) when they are greene, is not so good, but after they be well dryed and seasoned of themselves, then to bake them in the fire, and set them so straight and even that an arrow cannot surpasse them, is excellent; then you may take off the upper rinde, and what with the smoake, and their own age, their colour will be so darke that they will give no reflect into the Water, (which is a principall observation).

Your Rod being made thus straight and seasoned, you shall at the upper end thereof, with an Augure or a hot Iron, but a hot Iron is the better, burne a hole about three inches deep, and of a fingers widenesse: then on the outside of the Rod, from the top of the hole unto the bottome, you shall warpt it about either with strong double twisted threed well waxed or pitcht, or with Shoo-makers threed many times doubled, and well waxed with Shooe-makers Wax, and the last end fastned under the last foulds, so close and so sure, that it may by no meanes loose; for this will keepe the Rod from cleaving or breaking in that same place, where the hollownesse was made.

The stock being thus made, you shall into the hole fix the Top, which would be a very small ground Hazell, growing from the Earth upward, very smooth and straight, which would be cut at the latter end of the yeare, and lie in season all the winter, the upper Rinde being by no means taken off, neyther the Rod put into the fire at all, but onely seasoned in a good dry place, where it may lie straight, and have both the Winde and some Ayre of the fire to come unto it. This Top must be plyant and bending, yet of such a sufficient strength, that it will not breake with any reasonable jerk, but as it is any way bowed, for to returne againe to the former straightnesse.

This top wand would be of a yard and a halfe, or an Ell at least in length, and at the smallest end thereof would be fastned with a warpe of haire, a strong loope of haire, about an inch long, to which you may at pleasure fasten your fishing line: and the bigger end of the top, must be thrust into the socket of the stock, and made so fast that it may not loosen nor shake out with any shaking, or other reasonable violence. And all be the Witchen or ground-elme are accounted the best to frame these maine stockes of, yet I have seene very good stockes made both of Sallow, Beech, or Poplar: for the lighter your Rod, is (so it be strong) it is so much the better, and more for the ease of him that useth it.

* * *

Now FOR your lines, you shall understand that they are to be made of the strongest, longest, and best growne Horse haire that can be got, not that which groweth on his mine, nor upon the upper part or setting on of his tayle, but that which groweth from the middle and in most part of his dock, and so extendeth itselfe down to the ground, being the biggest and strongest haires about the Horse: neither are these haires to be gathered from poore, leane, & diseased Jades of little price or value, but from the fattest, soundest, and proudest Horse you can fine, for the best Horse hath ever the best hayre; neither would your hayres be gathered from Nagges, Mares, or Geldings, but from ston'd-Horses onely, of which the black haire is the worst, the white or gray best, and other colours indifferent.

Those lines which you make for small Fish, as Gudgeon, Witling, or Menow, would bee composed of three hayres; those which you make for *The* Pearch, or Trout, would be of five hayres; and those for the chub or Barbell, would be of seaven. To those of three hayres you shall add one threed of silke; to those of five *Haire* two threeds of silke; and to those of seaven three threeds of silke. You shall twist your hayres neither too hard nor too slacke, but even so as they may twinde and coutch *Line* close one within another and no more, without either snarling or gaping on from another: the end, you shall fasten together with a Fishers knot, which is your ordinary fast knot, foulded foure times about, both under and above, for this will not loose in the water, but being drawne close together will continue when all other knots will faile, for a hayre being smooth and stiffe, will yeeld and goe backe if it bee not artificially drawne together.

Your ordinary Line would be betweene three and foure fadome in length, yet for as much as there are diversities in the length of Rods, in the depth of waters, and in the places of standing to Angle in, it shall be good to have Lines of divers lengths, and to take those which shall be fittest.

YOUR HOOKES bee of divers shapes and fashions, some bigge, some little, some between both, according to the Fish at which you angle, the best substance whereof to make them is either old Spanish Needles, or els strong wyer drawne as neere as may be to that hight of termpers, which being nealed and alayde in the fire, you may bend and bow at your pleasure.

Now for the best softning of your Wyer, if you make your Hookes of old Needles, you shall neede but to hold them in the blaze of a Candle till they bee red hot, and then let them coole of themselves, and they will be soft, and plyant enough, but if you make your Hookes of strong Spanish Wyer, you shall roule it rounde, and then lay it upon burning Char-Coales, turning it up and downe till it bee all red hot in every place, then let it gently coole of it selfe, and it will bee soft enough.

The

Hooke

Now for the making of your Hookes, I advise you to goe to such as are best reputed for making of them, and buy of all sorts of Hookes from the biggest to the least, that is to say, from that which taketh the Loach, to that which taketh the Salmon, and let them lye before you for examples: then look of what sort of Hookes you intend to make, and with a fine File, first make the poynt of your Hooke, which would neyther bee too sharpe, for then it will catch hold of everything, when it should not, nor too blunt, least it faile to take hold when there is occasion: thereforein that observe a meane, making it lesse sharpe then a fine Needle, and more sharpe than a small Pinne.

When you have made the poynt then with a thinne Knife of a very good edge, you shall cut out and raise up the berd which you shall make greater or lesse, according to the binesse of the Hooke, and the strength of the Whyre: for you must by no meanes cut the beard so deepe, that thereby you weaken the Hooke, but it must bee as strong in that place as any other.

When the poynt and beard is made, you shall with a fine paire of round Plyers turne and compasse, the Hooke about, making it round, circular-wise, being somewhat more then a semicircle, and ever observe that the rounder the compasse or bought commeth in, that so much the better pro-portioned the Hooke is.

This done, you shall leave as much as you thinke convenient for the shanke, and then cut it off from the rest of the Wyer: which done, you shall beate the end downe flat, and somewhat broader then the rest, and so pollish and smooth it all over, then heating it red hot in a little Panne of Charchoales put it suddenly into the Water, and quench it, which will bring your Hooke to a full strength and hardness.

Thus you see how to make Hookes of all sizes and shapes, whether they be single or double Hookes, for although the quantities alter, yet the shaipes do not; and the double Hooke which is the Pile-hooke, is no other, but two singel Hookes all of one Wyer, turned contrary wayes.

IT NOW resteth that wee speake of other necessary implements, which shaould accompany the painefull and insistrious Angler, and they bee these: Hee shall besides these before spoken of, have a large musket bullet, through which having fixed a double twisted threed, and thereof made a strong loope, he may at his pleasure hang it upon his Hooke, and therewith sound the depth of every water, and so know how to plumbe his lines, and place his corke in their due places, then hee shall have a large ring of lead, six

Other Imple- ments

inches at least in compasse, and made fast to a small long line, through which, thrusting your Angle rod, and letting it fall into the Water by your haire Line, it will help to undo your Hooke if it be fastned, either upon weeks or other stones in the Water.

Then he shall have a fine smooth board of some curious Wood for shew sake, being as big as a Trencher, and cut battlement-wise at each end, on which hee shall fold his severall Lines, hiss hokkes he shall have in a dry close box; hee shall have a little Bag of red cloath, to carry his Wormes in, and mix with them a little fresh mould and Fennel; then he shall either have a close stopt Horne, in which he shall keep Maggots, Bobbes, Palmers, and such like or a hollow Cane, in which he may put them, and Scarrabs.

He shall have a close box for all sorts of live flies, and another for Needles, Silke, Threed, Wax, and loose haires, then a role of pitch Threed to mend the Angle rod withall, if it chance to break, a File, a Knife, a Pouch with many purses, in which you may place all your implements whatsoever severally.

Lastly, hee shall have a little fine wanded Pebbe to hang by his side, in which he shall put the Fish he catcheth, and a small round Net fastned

The Angler's Clothes

unto a paoles end, wherewith hee may land a Pike, or any other great Fish of that kinde whatsoever.

TOUCHING the Angler's appareell (for it is a sespect as necessary as any other whatsoever) it would by no means be garish, light coloured, or shining, for whatsoever with a glittering hew it reflecteth upon the water, immediately it frighteth the Fish, and maketh them flie from his presence, no hunger being able to tempt them to bite, when their eye is offended.

Let then your appareell be plaine and comely, or a darke colour, as Russet, Tawny, or such like, close to your body, without any new fashioned flashes or dangling sleeves, waving loose, like sailes about you, for they are like Blinks which will ever chase your Game from you: let it for your owne health and ease sake, bee warms and well lined, that neither the colnesse of the Ayre, nor the moistnesse of the water may offend you.

Keep your head and feet dry, for from the offence of them springeth Agues and worse infirmities.

Gervase Markham, 1568-1637: COUNTRY CONTENTMENTS.

BEYOND ANY HAIR FOR STRENGTH AND SMALLNESS

MARCH 18th, 1667. This day Mr. Caesar told me a pretty experiment of his, of angling with a minnikin, a gut-string varnished over, which keeps it from swelling, and is beyond any hair for strength and smallness. The secret I like mightily.

Samuel Pepys: DIARY, 1667.

A CHEERFUL WIFE TO BITE THE SHOT

EVERY Roach angler who fishes with hair should take with him half a dozen hair-hooks, shotted for immediate use . . . and should he be blessed with a pretty and cheerful wife, who could sacredly be trusted to bite the shot on properly, the writer feels that hooks so shotted must prove the luckiest.

What a mistake Roach anglers, who have sons and daughters, make in not training their children early to be useful in this sport. The sons in the proper making up of paste and ground-bait, the daughters in the manufacturing of nets, the thorough knowledge of fishermen's knots, whipping, and how properly to tie on Roach and other hooks.

Henry Wix, 1860. Mr. Wix was treasurer of St. Bartholomew's hospital.

A BOY TO GO ALONG

WHENEVER you go out to Fish, faill not to have with you, *viz:*

A good Coat for all Weathers.

An *Apron* to put your *Ground-Bait, Stones,* and *Paste* in.

A Basket to put your *Fish* in.

A neat *Rod* of about four Foot long, in several pieces, one within another.

Two or three Lines fitted up, of all Sorts.

Spare *Hooks, Links, Floats, Silk, Wax, Plummetts, Caps,* and a *Landing Nett,* etc.

And if you have a Boy to go along with you, a good *Cow's-Tongue,* and a Bottle of *Canary* should not be wanting: To the enjoyment of which I leave you.

William Gilbert: THE ANGLER'S DELIGHT, 1676.

NEITHER HOOK NOR LINE

You see the ways the fisherman doth take
To catch the fish; what engines doth he make?
Behold! how he engageth all his wits;
Also his snares, lines, angles, hooks and nets;
Yet fish there be, that neither hook nor line,
Nor snare, nor net, nor engine, can make thine:
They must be groped for, and be tickled too,
Or they will not be catch'd, whate'er you do.

John Bunyan, 1628-1689.

123

Baits & Flies

LIVE BAITES, DEAD BAITES & BAITES LIVING IN APPARENCE ONELY

To SPEAKE then generally of Baites, they are divided into three kinds, which are, live baites, Dead-baites, & Baites living but in apparence onely.

Your live baits are wormes of all kindes, especiall the Red-worm, the Maggot, the Bobbe, the Dor, browne Flyes, Frogs, Grashoppers, Hornets, Waspes, Bees, Snailes, small Roaches, Bleades, Glodgins, or Loches.

Your dead Baites are pastes of all makings, your brood of Wasps dried or undried, the clotted blood of Sheepe, Cheese, Bramble-berries, Corne, Seedes, Cherries, and such like.

And your Baites which seem to Live, yet are Dead, are Flyes artificially made of all sorts and shapes, made of silke and Feathers about your Hookes, which well serve for every several seasons through the yeare, and being by your Line moved upon the water, seems to be live Flies, which the fish with great greedinesse will catch up and devoure.

Gervase Markham, 1568-1637: COUNTRY CONTENTMENTS.

125

BEG THE MAID TO MAKE GROUND BAIT

Go to Mother *Gibert's* at the *Flower-de-Luce* at *Clapton*, near *Hackney*, and whilst you are drinking of a Pot of *Ale*, beg the Maid make you two or three Peny-worth of *Ground Bait*, and some *Paste* (which they do very neatly, and well); and observing of them, you will know how to make it yourself for any other Place; which is too tedious here to Insert.

William Gilbert: THE ANGLER'S DELIGHT, 1676.

THE NAKED FRAUD

You must not ev'ry worm promiscuous use,
Judgment will tell thee proper bait to choose;
The worm that draws a long immod'rate size
The trout abhors, and the rank morsel flies;
And if too small, the naked fraud's in sight,
And fear forbids, while hunger does invite.

John Gay: RURAL SPORTS, 1713.

GOOSE GREASE AND DEAD MAN'S SCULL

Take a fat goose or Duck, pluck and draw it, then take sage, marjoram, and french lavender, of each a like quantity, and shred it small: of castor, Gum-armoniack, calamus aromaticus, Nutmeg, Mace, and Cloves, of each a little, beat the Spices well in a Mortoar, then mix them with your shred Herbs, and put them into the Belly of the Goose or duck; sew up the belly close, rost him on a Spit, and save the dripping fat for your use, and eat the Goose or Duck for your pains.

When you have occasion, take a quantity of the Fat that dript from him, and mix it well with oyl of a dead man's scull, and oyl of Earthworms and yse the ointment for the arming of your hook, then fix six or eight inches of your Line next above the hook, and then dip your bait in it after it's on the hook, and fish.

Robert Howlett: THE ANGLER'S SURE GUIDE, 1706.

BAYTES FOR GRETE FYSSHE

FOR BAYTES for grete fysshe, kepe especyally this rule: whan ye haue take a grete fysshe: vndo the mawe: & what ye fynde therein, make that your bayte: for it is beste.

THE BOKE OF ST. ALBANS, 1496.

COMFORTABLE TO THE BRAIN

AMBERGRISE, some say, is a sweet Aromatick Juice or Perfume but Aetius and Simeon Sethius, Greek authors, affirm it to be a kind of Bitumen, coming forth of the Fountains of Springs in the bottom of the Sea, and by floating on the Saltwater, becomes condensate or thickned, still retaining its original oyliness: a great quantity thereof is found in Sofala, and in the Isles of Comaro, Demogra, Mosambique, and along this tract, even to the Isles of Maldina, or Naledina, which look into the East.

There is Amber-grise of four several colours, gray, white, red and black, which comes according to the variety of places or regions where it is found; the gray, i.e., of the colour of wood ashes or of ashcolour, is preferred before all other, and is known to be right good, if, when pricking it with a Pin, it puts forth a Moisture like Oyl; is not ponderous, but light, and of good Scent; it is hot and dry in the second degree, and very comfortable to the brain.

Robert Howlett: THE ANGLER'S SURE GUIDE, 1706.

TAKE OF MAN'S FAT

MONSIEUR CHARRAS, Apothecary royal to the late French King, Lewis the Fourteenth, says: "Take of man's fat* and cat's fat, of each half an ounce; mummy, finely powdered, three drams; cumminseed, finely powdered one dram; distilled oil of aniseed and spite, of each six drops; civet, two grains; and camphire, four grains: make an ointment according to art."

When you angle with this, anoint eight inches of the line next the hooke; because if you angle with one hair it will not stick so well to the line."

Greville Fennel. CURIOSITIES OF ANGLING LITERATURE (DATE UNKNOWN).
* For "man's fat" the reader is directed to any surgeon. E. B.

TO MAKE THE FISH TO BITE

Wouldst thou catch Fish?
Then here's thy wish;
Take this receipt,
To annoynt thy Baite.
Thou that desir'st to fish with Line and Hooke,
Be it in poole, in riuer, or in Brooke,
To blisse thy baite, and make the Fish to bite;
Loe, here's a meanes, if thou can'st hit it right.
Take Gum of life, fine beate and laid in soake
In Oyle, well drawne from that which kils the Oake.
Fish where thou wilt, thou shalt haue sport thy fill,
When twenty faile, thou shalt be sure to kill.

Probatum.

Its perfect and good,
If well understood;
Else not to be tolde
For siluer or golde.

B. R.

John Dennys: SECRETS OF ANGLING, 1613.

EMPTY BASKETS CHANGE THE TUNE

The good March Brown in April, May,
Your labour sweet will better pay,
But when the pink wild roses blow
Or heather blooms, 'tis time to show
The blue-nosed worm.

"The thing's amiss," some critics sneer;
" 'Tis dirty work and torture sheer,"
Yet empty baskets change their tune,
And they discard, in leafy June,
The fly, for worm.

Alexander Mackie: THE ART OF WORM-FISHING, 1912.
(A. and C. Black, Ltd.)

THOU ART THINE OWNE BAIT

Come liue with me and be my loue,
And we will some new pleasure proue,
Of golden sands and cristall brooks,
With silken lines and siluer hooks.

There will the riuer whisperinge runne
Warm'd by thine eyes more then the sunne;
And there th' inamor'd fish will stay,
Begginge themselues they may betray.

When thou wilt swimme in that liue bath,
Each fish, which euery channell hath
Will amorously to thee swimme,
Gladder to catch thee than thou him.

If thou to be so seen beest loath
By sunne or moone, thou darknest both;
And if myselfe haue leaue to see,
I need not their light, hauing thee.

Let others freeze with anglinge reeds,
And cutt their leggs with shells and weeds,
Or treacherously poore fish besett
With stranglinge snare or windinge nett:

Let coarse bold hands, from slimy nest,
The bedded fish in bancks outwrest,
Or curious traitors, sleaue-silk flies,
Bewitch poore fishes' wanderinge eyes.

For thee, thou needst no such deceit,
For thou thyself art thine owne bait:
That fish that is not catch'd thereby,
Alas, is wiser farr than I!

John Donne: POEMS BY J.D., 1633.

129

HAIRS OF BAIRS

ALWAYS make your Dub-flies on a Sunshine Day; and to know the exact colour of your dubbing, hold the same betwixt your Eye and the Sun, and you'll far better discover the true colour of the dubbing, than only by looking on it in the Hand, in the House, dark Day, or a shady Place.

Some always advise to dub with Silk of the most predominant colour of the Fly; but we generally dub Duns with Yellow Silk, and our Browns with Red Silk, and at *September* with Violet Silk, or Horseflesh coloured Silk.

Flies made of the Hair of Bairs, Hogs, Squirrels Tail, Camels, Dogs, Foxes, Badgers, Otters, Ferrets, Cow, Calves Skins tewed; abortive Calves and Colts Skins tewed, Weasels, Outlandish Caddows, etc., are more natural, lively, and keep colour better in the Water than Flies made of Crewels, and many sort of Worsted stuffs, which are of a dead and dull colour in the Water, therefore to be eschewed, unless you mingle Hairs of Bairs, or Hogs therewith.

James Chetham: THE ANGLER'S VADE MECUM, 1681.

FLIES PROPER TO THE PLACE

THERE are peculiar flies proper to the particular place or country; and doubtless, unless a man makes a fly to counterfeit that very fly in that place, he is like to lose his labor, or much of it: but for the generality, three or four flies neat and rightly made, and not too big, serve for a Trout in most rivers all the summer.

Izaak Walton: THE COMPLETE ANGLER, 1653.

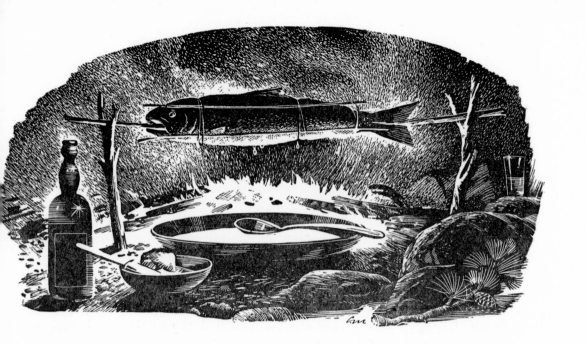

Fish On The Table

THOROUGHLY DONE

LET all fish that are roasted, boil'd, stew'd, fry'd, broil'd or baked be thoroughly done.

Robert Howlett, THE ANGLER'S SURE GUIDE, 1706.

SO LET IT STEW

TAKE a large Trout fair Trim'd and Wash it, put it into a large Pewter dish then take half a pint of sweet Wine, with a lump of Butter, and a little Mace, Parsley, Savory and Thyme, mince them all small, and put them into the belly of the Trout, and so let it stew a quarter of an Hour, then mince the yolk of an hard Egg, and strew it on the Trout, lay the Herbs about it. Scrape on sugar and serve it up.

Anonymous.

THROW AWAY THE BONES AND INTERIOR

Now shall you see some real sportsman's Cookery. "Give me half-a-dozen of those perch, Patsey, and that copy of the *Times* newspaper."
Now observe me.

Take each perch separately, namely wiping him dry—not cutting or scraping him in the least, as that would break the skin and let out his juices;—then take a piece of paper, and wet it in the lake, and roll the perch in it, in three or four folds; screw up the ends, and thrust perch, paper and all, into the embers.

In from five to ten minutes, your fish is cooked. Rake him out; take off the charred paper, and carefully remove his scales, which will come off *en masse;* rub the white succulent side with butter; pepper and salt, to taste; make an incision along the backbone, and flake off all the beautiful firm white flesh; turn the carcase over and serve the other side of the fish in the same way; throw away the bones and interior; and eat the remainder.

It is a dish for a king, or an angler.

Francis Francis: A MONTH IN THE WEST, 1886.
(The Field Magazine)

QUICKEN THEIR AFFECTIONS TO ANGLING

Now for as mauch as many Anglers themselves may not only be ignorant of a well dressing the fish they catch, but may when abroad a fishing, frequently fall into such Quarters where they may meet as little Knowledge as they themselves have; to supply that defect, I shall furnish them with such variety of Receipts in the end of every Chapter to dress the Fish there treated of, as may yield Delight both to them and their Friends in eating the Fruits of their Labours, and quicken their affections the more to the lovely Recreation of Angling.

Robert Howlett: THE ANGLER'S SURE GUIDE, 1706.

SPRING LIKE A FLEA

FISH-DINNERS will make a man spring like a flea.

Thomas Jordan, 1612-1685: CORONEMUS NOS ROSIS ANTEQUAM MARCESCANT.

WILL EAT WELL HOT OR COLD

GUT, gill, and wash your trouts clean, and dry them with a clean Linen-cloth, both inside and outside; then lay butter in your pie, and your

Trout

Pie

fish upon it, some whole cloves, mace and flicked nutmeg, with two handfuls of capers, currans, clean washed and cullender'd; then mix some butter with salt, and lay it over all, and lit it; immediately before it's set in the Oven, put in some white wine at the vent hole and bake it.

Anonymous

ROAST THE GREAT TROUT LEISURELY

WIPE him well with a dry clean cloth, then slit him one inch at the upper end of his belly, close to the head, or gills; and likewise as much within one Inch of his Vent, leaving the Belly uncut between the two slits; by which means you may take his intrails clean out; then wash him, keeping the rest of his belly whole; which done, take half a pound of fresh butter, a quantity of Thyme, sweet Marjoram and Parsley, all chopt small; mix the Butter unmelted, and Herbs together, and put them into his Belly, with half a dozen oysters; then sew up the two slits.

Roast

Trout

If you have not a spit made for the purpose spit him on a common broach, not too big, and thrust it quite through the Fish, in at mouth, and out at Tail: then place four or five, or more slit sticks, or small, thin narrow Laths, full as long as the Fish, upon the Fish, round about him, and wind as much Pack-thread or rather broad tape about the sticks or laths, fish and spit, as will bind him fast to the spit, and keep him from falling off.

Lay him to a good clear fire, and rost him leisurely; first basting him with Claret wine, then with fresh butter and an Anchove beaten well together, and after that with the liquor that falls from the Fish, till he be rosted enough; then take a very warm dish, which cause to be held under the fish; and having unwound, or cut the pack-thread, or Tape, and cut open the trouts belly, that he may fall into the Dish without further trouble.

Then beat up what dripp'd from him, with what you rosted in his belly, with some frest Butter for sawce, and add to it the juice of three or four Oranges, and pour all on the Fish, and serve it up.

Anonymous

COOK GENTLY IN THE WISE FASHION

I WILL pass you on the closely-treasured and cherishly-guarded recipe I had from the descendant of one Fria Convivius—who I sincerely hope is in heaven—and which was one of the delights of Madame Juliane de Berners, who wrote the first book on 'Fyshing with an Angle' in 1496, and who had it from the winsome sister who kept the Refectory of the Nunery.

Gather a pound or so of mushrooms when the dew lies heavy on the cap, catch your bream before the sun can scorch its sides, lay it in salt and bay leaves till two hours passes noon, and then having cleaned, scaled and taken out the throat, and all that therein is, lay it in a wide dish of clay or earthenware with a goodly sprinkle of thyme, rosemary, marjoram, mace, and the mushrooms; stiffening it with forcemeat made of liver and pig's flesh, fat, and some of the herbs with a chopped shallot all mixed with breadcrumbs.

Place pieces of butter on the top of the bream, and stew in the oven—basting with a rich brown sauce made of some of the liver and pig's flesh with a beaker of malvoisie—half a glass of any wine will do in these less romantic days—and cook gently in the wise fashion taught by samplers of the monastic court.

A. M. Young, 1864-1926: THE STORY OF THE STREAM.

SO EXCELLENTLY COOKED THIS FISH

VENATOR: Why, Sir, it is that from henceforth you would allow me to call you Master, and that really I may be your scholar; for you are such a companion, and have so quickly caught and so excellently cooked this fish, as makes me ambitious to be your scholar.

PISCATOR: Give me your hand; from this time forward I will be your master, and teach you as much of this art as I am able; and I am sure I both can and will tell you more than any common Angler yet knows.

Izaak Walton: THE COMPLEAT ANGLER, 1653.

Food & Lodging

SOUR BEER

I MAY possibly be the means of saving some of our young sportsmen, or young "foragers," from unnecessarily hard fare, when quartered in a small public-house, on some shooting or fishing excursion.

As many of the little publicans live chiefly on fat pork and tea; or, if on the coast, red herrings; the experienced traveller well knows, that, when in a retired place of this sort, where, from the very circumstance of the misery attending it, there are the fewer sportsmen, and, consequently, there is to be had the best diversion, we have often to depend a little on our wits for procuring the necessaries of life.

If even a nobleman (who is, of course, by common people, thought in the greatest extreme better than a gentleman without a title) were to enter an alehouse, the most that could be procured for him would be mutton or beef, both perhaps as tough, and with as little fat, as the boots or gaiters on his legs. A chop or steak is provided. If he does not eat it, he may starve; if he does, his pleasure for the next day is possibly destroyed by his unpleasant sufferings from indigestion. He gets some sour beer, which gives him the heartburn, and probably calls for brandy, or gin; the one execrably bad and unwholesome; the other of the worst quality; and, *of course,* mixed with water, by which adulteration is derived the greatest part of the publican's profit. The spirit merchants make it, what they call above proof, in order to allow for its being *diluted,* the doing which, so far from dishonesty, is now the common practice, not only with many respectable innkeepers, but by retail merchants themselves.

Our young sportsman, at last, retires to a miserable chamber and a worse bed; where, for want of ordering it to be properly aired, he gets the rheumatism; and, from the draughts of air that penetrate the room, he is attacked with the tooth-ache.

He rises to a breakfast of bad tea, without milk; and then starts for his day's sport, so (to use a fashionable term) "bedevilled" that he cannot "touch a feather": and, in the evening, returns to his second edition of misery.

Col. Peter Hawker: INSTRUCTIONS TO YOUNG SPORTSMEN, 1814.

KEEPING BUSY IN THE POTHOUSE WHEN IT RAINS

HAVING now said enough as to taking care of, and providing for, my young readers, we will suppose one of them to have arrived at the miserable hole alluded to, and that the first salutation, after the knock at his bed-chamber door, in the morning, is: *"A wet day, sir!"* And, instead of being able to pursue his sport, either after breakfast, or at noon *(the most usual time for the weather to clear up,* if it clears up at all), he is consigned a close prisoner to the pothouse; looking alternately to the windward clouds, and the plastered walls of the room; hearing, through a thin partition, the discordant merriment of drunken fellows; and inhaling the breezes of a smoky wood fire, with the fumes of their shag tobacco!

In such a predicament, then, how can I prescribe for him? And in this predicament, I believe, there are very few sportsmen that have not often been.

Why here again, then, I will endeavor to give him a little advice, though I hope he will not think I am beginning to write a sermon.

I shall now first observe, that, of all things on earth, to make a man low-spirited, unhappy, or *nervous,* is to get into a habit, of *idleness;* and although there are many young people that would pay little attention, and perhaps laugh at me, if I told them that "Idleness" was the "root of all evil," yet some, among those very persons, might listen most earnestly, when I remind them, that being *nervous* or *low-spirited* is of all other things the most likely to put even a crack *sportsman* off *his shooting;* or to make a young angler *whip off his flies; or be too eager, and therefore unskilful, in killing his fish.* Always, therefore, let him be *employed,* and think no more of the weather, till his man comes, with a smiling face, and says, *"Sir, it will do again now!"* when, if he is a man of genius, and has proper resources, he could almost have wished for another hour's rain, in order to complete that in which his mind was become absorbed.

Supposing the hole in which, for the sake of a few days' good sport, he is immured, contains neither books, nor newspapers; nor even stationery good enough to write a few letters in comfort (which, by the way, he should always be enabled to do, by carrying a quire of paper, and one of Clay's new steel pens), still there is no excuse for his being in *sheer idleness.* The mere pocket will always contain enough to employ successfully many a leisure hour. If he is studying any thing particular, he may be provided with some little volume, the most useful to his subject. If he draws, he may, at least, make a sketch of the hole he is in, for a laugh when he gets home; or, if in another style, practise, according to his fancy. If he is a "musician," and away from an instrument, let him learn to do some exercises in harmony. If he is an author or a poet, he can never be at a loss; or, if nothing greater, perhaps he may be a merry fellow, who sings a good song over his bottle, and therefore, on this occasion, by being provided with a "Pocket Nightingale," he may stock himself with songs enough to enliven all his associates on his return.

Col. Peter Hawker: INSTRUCTIONS TO YOUNG SPORTSMEN, 1814.

A BRAVE BREAKFAST

Go YOU to yonder sycamore-tree, and hide your bottle of drink under the hollow root of it; for about that time, and in that place, we will make a brave breakfast with a piece of powdered beef, and a radish or two that I have in my fish-bag: we shall, I warrant you, make a good, honest, wholesome, hungry breakfast; and I will then give you direction for the making and using of your flies: and in the mean time there is your rod and line; and my advice is, that you fish as you see me do, and let's try which can catch the first fish.

Izaak Walton: THE COMPLEAT ANGLER, 1653.

The Bookshelf

MY LITTLE BOOK

To the
Right Honourable Edward Lord Montague,
    Generall of the Navy, and one of the Lords Commissioners of the
       Treasury.
Noble Lord,

I do present this my book as I have named it, *Barker's Delight,* to your Honour. I pray God send you safe home to your good Lady and sweet Babes. *Amen, Amen.*

If you shall find anything delightfull in the reading of it, I shall heartily rejoyce, for I know you are one who takes delight in that pleasure, and have good judgement and experience, as many noble persons and Gentlemen of true piety and honour do and have. The favour that I have found from you, and a great many more that did and do love that pleasure, shall never be bury'd in oblivion by me.

I am now grown old, and am willing to enlarge my little book. I have written no more but mine own experience and practice, and have set forth the true ground of Angling, which I have been gathering these three score years, having spent many pounds in the gaining of it, as is well known in the place where I was born and educated, which is *Bracemeale* in the Liberty of *Salop*, being a Freeman and Burgesse of the same City.

If any noble or gentle Angler, of what degree soever he be, have a mind to discourse of any of these wayes and experiments, I live in *Henry* the 7th's Gifts, the next doore to the Gatehouse in *Westm.*, my name is *Barker*, where I shall be ready, as long as please God, to satisfie them, and maintain my art, during life, which is not like to be long; that the younger fry may have my experiments at a smaller charge than I had them, for, it would be too heavy for every one that loveth that exercise to be at that charge as I was at first in my youth, the losse of my time, with great expences.

Therefore I took it in consideration, and thought fit to let it be understood, and to take pains to set forth the true grounds and wayes that I have found by experience both for the fitting of rods and tackles both for ground-baites and flyes, with directions for the making thereof, with observations for times and seasons, for the ground-baites and flyes, both for day and night, with the dressing, wherein I take as much delight as in the taking of them, and to show how I can perform it, to furnish any Lords table, onely with trouts, as it is furnished with flesh, for 16 to 20 dishes. And I have a desire to preserve their health (with help of God) to go dry in their boots and shooes in angling, for age taketh the pleasure from me.

My Lord, I am

Your Honours most humble Servant,

THOMAS BARKER.

Thomas Barker: BARKER'S DELIGHT, 1657.

I HAVE MADE MYSELF A RECREATION OF A RECREATION

I WISH the reader to take notice, that in writing of it (the discourse) I have made myself a recreation of a recreation; and that it might prove so to him, and not read dull and tediously, I have in several places mixed, not any scurrility, but some innocent, harmless mirth, of which, if thou be severe, sour-complexioned man, then I here disallow thee to be a competent judge; for divines say there are *offences given,* and *offences not given but taken.*

And I am the willinger to justify the pleasant part of it, because, though it is known, I can be serious at seasonable times, yet the whole Discourse is, or rather was, a picture of my own disposition, especially in such days and times as I have laid aside business, and gone a-fishing with honest Nat. and R. Roe; but they are gone, and with them most of my pleasant hours, even as a shadow that passeth away and returns not.

Izaak Walton: THE COMPLEAT ANGLER, 1653.

READING OLD IZAAK

FOR my part, I was always a bungler at all kinds of sport that required either patience or adroitness, and had not angled for above half an hour before I had completely "satisfied that sentiment," and convinced myself of the truth of Izaak Walton's opinion, that angling is something like poetry —a man must be born to it. I hooked myself instead of the fish; tangled my line in every tree; lost my bait; broke my rod; until I gave up the attempt in despair, and passed the day under the trees, reading old Izaak; satisfied that it was his fascinating vein of honest simplicity and rural feeling that had bewitched me, and not the passion for angling. My companions, however, were more persevering in their delusion. I have them at this moment before my eyes, stealing along the border of the brook, where it lay open to the day, or was merely fringed by shrubs and bushes.

I recollect, also that, after toiling and watching and creeping about for the greater part of a day, with scarcely any success, in spite of all our admirable apparatus, a lubberly country urchin came down from the hills with a rod made from the branch of a tree, a few yards of twine, and, as Heaven shall help me! I believe, a crooked pin for a hook, baited with a vile earth-worm—and in half an hour caught more fish than we had nibbles throughout the day!

But, above all, I recollect the "good, honest, wholesome, hungry" repast which we made under a beech-tree, just by a spring of pure sweet water that stole out of the side of the hill; and how, when it was over, one of the party read old Izaak Walton's scene with the milkmaid, while I lay on the grass and built castles in a bright pile of clouds, until I fell asleep.

Washington Irving: THE SKETCH BOOK, 1820.

WALTON IS TO BE PITIED (POOR MAN)

FOR indeed the frequent exercise of fly-fishing, though painful, yet it's delightful, more especially when managed by the methods of art, and the practical rules and mediums of artists. But the ground-bait was of old the general practice, and beyond dispute brought considerable profit; which hapned in those days, when the curiosity of fly-fishing was intricate and unpracticable.

However Isaac Walton (late author of the *Compleat Angler*) has imposed upon the world this monthly novelty, which he understood not himself; but stuffs his book with morals from Dubravius and others, not giving us one precedent of his own practical experiments, except otherwise where he prefers the trencher before the troling-rod; who lays the stress of his arguments upon other men's observations, wherewith he stuffs his indigested octavo; so brings himself under the angler's censure, and the common calamity of a plagiary, to be pitied (poor man) for his loss of time, in scribling and transcribing other men's notions.

These are the drones that rob the hive, yet flatter the bees that bring them honey.

Richard Franck: NORTHERN MEMOIRS, 1694.

THOSE OLD BOOKS

"YES, I see you looking at those old books. Truly, there they are. Old Leonard Mascall's *Booke of Fishing with Hook and Line, and all other instruments thereunto belonging, &c., &c.,* printed in black letter by John Wolfe, in London, in 1590, sixty-three years before his next-door neighbor, dear old Izaak's *Complete Angler*. There they are, the whole five editions, in good preservation, and the original binding too; worth 30*l*. and more in the market any day. There, too, on the other side is old Gervase Markham's *Country Contentments*, with its quaint notion on fishing, only forty years anterior to Izaak. There they all are, up to the days of Blaine, Hawker, Ronalds, Ephemera, and other moderns, over whom, my dear boy, we will draw a veil.

Francis Francis: HOT POT: OR MISCELLANEOUS PAPERS, 1880.
(The Field Magazine)

THE PLEASURE WALTON HAS GIVEN

I SHALL expect you to bring me a brimful account of the pleasure which Walton has given you, when you come to town. It must square with your mind. The delightful innocence and healthfulness of the Angler's mind will have blown upon yours like a Zephyr.

Don't you already feel your spirit *filled* with the scenes?—the banks of rivers—the cowslip beds—the pastoral scenes—the neat alehouses—and hostesses and milkmaids, as far exceeding Virgil and Pope as the *Holy Living* is beyond Thomas a Kempis. Are not the eating and drinking joys painted to the Life? Do they not inspire you with an immortal hunger? Are you not ambitious of being made an Angler?

What edition have you got? Is it Hawkins's, with plates of Piscator, etc.? That sells very dear. I have only been able to purchase the last edition without the old Plates which pleased my childhood; the plates being worn out, and the old Edition difficult and expensive to procure.

The *Complete Angler* is the only Treatise written in Dialogues that is worth a halfpenny. Many elegant dialogues have been written (such as Bishop Berkeley's *Minute Philosopher*), but in all of them the Interlocutors are merely abstract arguments personify'd; not living dramatic characters, as in Walton, where *every thing* is *alive;* the fishes are absolutely *charactered;* and birds and animals are as interesting as men and women.

Charles Lamb: LETTERS, 1801. Written to Robert Lloyd, Feb., 7, 1801.

THE MOST PERFECT AND COMPLEAT TREATISE

I MAY, without Vanity, affirm, that this Treatise upon *Angling,* is the most *perfect* and *compleat* of any that has hitherto appeared in print.

George Smith: THE GENTLEMAN ANGLER, 1726.

Be quiet, and go a-Angling.

Izaak Walton: THE COMPLEAT ANGLER, 1653.

Acknowledgments

Author	Date	Title	Publishing House
Adamson, William Agar	1860	*Salmon Fishing in Canada*	Longmans Green and Co., Ltd.
Addison, Joseph	1672-1719	*The Spectator, No. 108*	
Aelfric	Roughly 1000 A.D.	*Colloquy, No. 53*	
Arnold, Matthew	1852	*Lines Written in Kensington Gardens*	The Macmillan Company
Audubon, John J.	1835	*Ornithological Biography*	E. L. Carey and A. Hart
Barker, Thomas	1657	*Barker's Delight*	
Barrie, James Matthew	1860-1937	*The Little Minister*	Charles Scribner's Sons
Bergman, Ray	1949	*Trout*	Alfred A. Knopf, Inc.
Boswell, James	1740-1795	*Life of Dr. Johnson*	
Bradley, John Hodgdon	1935	*Farewell Thou Busy World*	Primavera Press
Bradner, Enos	1950	*Northwest Angling*	A. S. Barnes and Co.
Breton, Nicholas	1604	*The Passionate Shepheard*	
Browning, Robert	1841	*Pippa Passes*	John Murray, Limited
Buchan, John (Lord Tweedsmuir)	1896	*Musa Piscatrix*	John Lane The Bodley Head, Ltd.
Bunyan, John	1628-1689	*(Excerpt: Neither Hook Nor Line)*	
Burns, Eugene	1952	*Advanced Fly Fishing*	
Buxton, Lord	1902	*Fishing and Shooting*	John Murray, Limited
Byron, Lord	1819-1824	*Don Juan*	Thomas Davison
Caine, William	1911	*An Angler at Large*	Routledge and Kegan Paul, Ltd.
Chalkhill, John	1653	*(Excerpt: The Best Life of Any)*	
Chaucer, Geoffrey	1340-1400	*The Compleynt of Mars*	
Chetham, James	1681	*The Angler's Vade Mecum*	
Churchill, George Bosworth	1924	*Miramichi Days*	Field & Stream Magazine
Clegg, Thomas	1950	*Running the Gadger*	Thomas Clegg
Cleveland, Grover	1906	*Fishing and Shooting Sketches*	The Macmillan Company
Connett, Eugene V., 3rd	1933	*Any Luck*	Doubleday & Co., Inc.
Cotton, Charles	1689	*Poems on Several Occasions*	
Curtis, Brian	1949	*The Life Story of the Fish*	Harcourt, Brace and Co.
D'Avenant, Sir William	1637	*Britannia Triumphans*	

AUTHOR	DATE	TITLE	PUBLISHING HOUSE
De la Mare, Walter	1873	*The Veil*	Henry Holt and Company, Inc.
Dennys, John	1613	*Secrets of Angling*	
Donne, John	1633	*Poems by J. D.*	
Doubleday, Thomas	1820	*Newcastle Fishers Garlands*	
Farson, Negley	1943	*Going Fishing*	Harcourt, Brace and Co., Inc.
Fennel, Greville	Unknown	*Curiosities of Angling*	
Field, Eugene	1850-1895	*(Excerpt: Our Biggest Fish)*	Charles Scribner's Sons
Fox, Charles K.	1950	*Advanced Bait Casting*	G. P. Putnam's Sons
Francis, Francis	1880	*Hot Pot: or Miscellaneous Papers*	The Field Magazine
Franck, Richard	1694	*Northern Memoirs*	
Froude, James Anthony	1818-1894	*Cheneys and the House of Russell*	Longmans Green and Co., Ltd.
Gay, John	1713	*Rural Sports*	
Gilbert, William	1676	*The Angler's Delight*	
Gilpatrick, Guy	1938	*The Compleat Goggler*	Dodd, Mead and Co.
Grey, Lord of Fallodon	1899	*Fly Fishing*	A. P. Watt and Son
Haig-Brown, Roderick L.	1946	*A River Never Sleeps*	William Morrow and Co., Inc.
Hawker, Col. Peter	1814	*Instructions to Young Sportsmen*	
Henderson, William	1879	*My Life As An Angler*	W. Satchell, Peyton and Co.
Hewitt, Edward Ringwood	1922	*A Trout and Salmon Fisherman for Seventy-five Years*	Charles Scribner's Sons
Hogg, James	1770-1835	*A Boy Loves to Play*	
Holland, Dan	1949	*Trout Fishing*	Thomas Y. Crowell Co.
Howlett, Robert	1706	*The Angler's Sure Guide*	
Hughes, Thomas	1857	*Tom Brown's Schooldays*	The Macmillan Company
Irving, Washington	1820	*The Sketch Book*	
Johnson, Dr. Samuel	1709-1784	*(Excerpt: A Worm At One End And A Fool At the Other)*	
Jordon, Thomas	1612-1685	*Coronemus Nos Rosis Antequam Marcescant*	
Kingsley, Charles	1856	*The Invitation*	The Macmillan Company
Knight, John Alden	1945	*The Theory and Technique of Fresh Water Angling*	Harcourt, Brace and Co., Inc.
Kreider, Claude M.	1948	*Steelhead*	G. P. Putnam's Sons
Lang, Andrew	1844-1912	*(Excerpt: The Contented Angler)*	Longmans Green and Co., Ltd.
Lamb, Charles	1801	*Letters, 1801*	
Lauson, William	1613	*Notes to Secrets of Angling by John Dennys*	
Leacock, Stephen	1936	*Here Are My Lectures*	Dodd, Mead and Co.
Lucas, Jason	1947	*On Bass Fishing*	Dodd, Mead and Co.
Mackie, Alexander	1912	*The Art of Worm-Fishing*	A. and C. Black, Ltd.
Markham, Gervase	1568-1637	*Country Contentments*	
Marquis, Don	1921	*Noah an' Jonah an' Cap'n John Smith*	Appleton-Century-Crofts, Inc.

ACKNOWLEDGMENTS

Author	Date	Title	Publishing House
Mascall, Leonard	1590	*A Booke of Fishing With Hooke and Line*	
Mather, Cotton	1702	*Magnalia Christi Americana*	
Mayer, John	1823	*The Sportsman's Directory*	
Milton, John	1608-1674	*Paradise Lost*	
Newbolt, Sir Henry	1912	*Poems: New and Old*	A. P. Watt and Son
Pepys, Samuel	1667	*Diary*	
Roxby, Robert	1820	*Newcastle Fishers' Garland*	
Scott, Sir Walter	1822	*Life in the Forest*	
Scrope, William	1843	*Days and Nights of Salmon Fishing*	James Blackwood and Co., Ltd.
Senior, William	1877	*By Stream and Sea*	Chatto and Windus, Ltd.
Shakespeare, William	1598	*Much Ado About Nothing*	
Sheringham, Hugh T.	1912	*Coarse Fishing*	A. and C. Black, Ltd.
Sheringham, Hugh T.	1920	*Trout Fishing*	Hodder and Stoughton
Skues, G. E. M.	1910	*Minor Tactics of the Chalk-Stream*	A. and C. Black, Ltd.
Smith, George	1726	*The Gentleman Angler*	
St. Albans, Boke of	1496	*(Excerpt: Fysshlynge Wyth an Angle)*	
Stevenson, Robert Louis	1850-1894	*To Andrew Lang*	The Society of Authors
St. John, The Apostle		*Cast to the Right*	
Stoddart, Thomas Tod	1866	*An Angler's Rambles*	James Blackwood and Co., Ltd.
Taverner, John	1600	*Certaine Experiments Concerning Fish and Fruite*	
Theoreau, Henry D.	1817-1862	*(Excerpt: Ktaadn Trout)*	Doubleday & Co., Inc.
Walton, Izaak	1653	*The Compleat Angler (xiii)*	
Washington, George	1789	*Washington's Diary*	
Wix, Henry	1860	*(Excerpt: A Cheerful Wife To Bite The Shot)*	
Wordsworth, William	1770-1850	*Written On A Blank Leaf*	
Young, A. M.	1864-1926	*The Story of the Stream*	